THE PLAY'S THE THING

THE PLAY'S THE THING

The Theatrical Collaboration of
Clark Bowlen and Kathleen Keena,

1988–2012

KATHLEEN KEENA

iUniverse

THE PLAY'S THE THING
THE THEATRICAL COLLABORATION OF CLARK BOWLEN
AND KATHLEEN KEENA, 1988–2012

iUniverse books may be ordered through booksellers or by contacting:

iUniverse
1663 Liberty Drive
Bloomington, IN 47403
www.iuniverse.com
1-800-Authors (1-800-288-4677)

ISBN: 978-1-4917-6151-9 (sc)
ISBN: 978-1-4917-6152-6 (e)

Library of Congress Control Number: 2015904646

Print information available on the last page.

iUniverse rev. date: 4/17/2015

The play's the thing
Wherein I'll catch the conscience of the king.
—William Shakespeare, *The Tragedy of Hamlet*, act 2, scene 11

CONTENTS

INTRODUCTION

I was a part-time college English teacher, Method-trained actor, and community director when I met Clark Bowlen, theater chair at Manchester Community College (MCC) in Connecticut, in 1988. We formed an artistic partnership that combined our diverse strengths to produce classic and contemporary shows. Actors joined us as fellow artists on a journey that spanned the academic, community, and theatricals worlds. Our work included a hip-hop *Midsummer Night's Dream*, a rock-and-roll *Taming of the Shrew*, a postwar-themed show performed by Vietnam veterans, and several original musicals. Nontraditional theater productions that addressed contemporary social issues became our signature work.

The purpose of this book is to document the nature and process of that work, to show how we developed a theater department at an ordinary community college and took it beyond the campus walls. Clark and I developed a professional partnership that expanded into a life commitment and marriage. After many years together, we anticipated a retirement filled with world travel and continuing our theater projects into old age. Unexpectedly, however, at sixty-five Clark was diagnosed with multiple systems atrophy, a terminal neurological disease that attacks and destroys the autonomic (involuntary) nervous system. Without warning, this insidious illness stole his vitality, paralyzed him, and abruptly ended our treasured artistic and personal life.

Thirteen years younger than Clark, I was fifty-seven when he died and was stunned by the loss. I now seek to document our collaboration for multiple reasons: to honor Clark for the magnificent artist he was; to celebrate our artistic partnership and the growth we both experienced in the process; and to document the ethereal nature of theater, how the significance of a project evaporates rapidly as the set is struck, and audience, cast, and crew leave the house. I want to honor the beauty of the creative process to those who might be considering a life in theater; Clark and I always hoped to impart that joy to actors, technicians, audience members, and everyone who helps make theater a reality. It is a personal and collaborative endeavor with the potential to challenge, engage, and acknowledge our imperfections. Finally, I hope to share my gratitude for our lifelong artistic collaboration.

This book explores three theater venues: academic, community, and independent. Clark and I developed our artistic style and approach within the academic realm and adapted our model when we moved into community and independent production.

Academia provided a freedom that we used to advance and expand the theater department at MCC. Clark, as theater chair, and I, as his in-house director, selected increasingly challenging productions that would not have drawn large popular audiences. Our scripts were literary and crossed historical and stylistic lines; they were best suited for English literature classes. Both of us preferred this type of theater and were comfortable and at home in academia. For thirteen years, we successfully ran a robust department despite the limitations the two-year college imposed on its theater program. In 2001, the department was eliminated due to overall college attrition. Clark remained in the college's Communications Division, teaching acting and speech. I moved to community theater, learning about its philosophy, artistic goals, audience composition, and rules of operation.

Two commonalities among community theaters are financial self-sufficiency and a tightly knit group of artists who hold certain assumptions about power, territory, and the limitations of production-specific personnel. In academic theater, the cast and crew were new every year. Community theaters, in contrast, often had people who had been with the company twenty or thirty years. Those individuals were the real organizational leaders and set the tone and attitude of the company.

Eventually, Clark and I realized that the power struggles that sometimes occur in less collaboratively based community theaters were a waste of creative energy, and we founded our own independent theater company. We gained the artistic control we had lost when the college theater program folded. However, running a theater company requires its own set of skills, including marketing, promotion, fundraising, recruiting cast and crew, locating performance and rehearsal spaces, and building an experienced company and a core audience. We were blissfully ignorant about a number of administrative challenges, such as filing for nonprofit status and managing the books. I am grateful we didn't know beforehand how nearly impossible this commitment would be. My best friend and mentor, theater director Barbara Kennedy, had just died of a brain tumor. Clark was only a few years away from losing his artistic and, ultimately, his entire life to a terminal disease. That we had the opportunity to found and operate a theater company was our ultimate success.

We'd come from different backgrounds but shared many producing, directing, and performance values. Clark's double major in design and directing at the University of Massachusetts (UMass) enhanced his background in classic and contemporary theater. He also was knowledgeable about the work of international directors and stage actors. That contrasted with my experience—training in Method acting at the Lee Strasberg Theatre and Film Institute in Hollywood, a directing apprenticeship with Barbara Kennedy in Los Angeles, and studies at Hartford Stage with actor and playwright Henry Thomas. Clark's experience was in fully conceptualized sets and complex lighting designs. I was at home with a bare stage, house lights, and character creation. I was fringe; he was traditional.

However, we both held English degrees. He had a minor in political science; mine was in social issues. We both had been business managers in our initial careers and entered education as a second profession. Clark had been active in community theater set design and lighting; I helped found—and acted, wrote, and directed for—Calliope Feminist Theater Company, a women's collective. We both loved Shakespeare.

When I saw Clark's first show, *Juno and the Paycock*, the set was uncluttered, with clean, understated simplicity. The actors really conversed with each other. They worked collectively; no one tried to upstage the others. The production values were exceptional, and I recognized that

Clark was a like-minded theater artist. I introduced myself as an actor, director, and part-time English instructor, and we scheduled a time to discuss play aesthetics. His emotional honesty, clarity, and originality convinced me that we ought to work together. For the next twenty-five years, until his death in 2012, we enjoyed a theatrical collaboration that was greater than anything we could have achieved individually. What united us was our mutual respect for and application of Method acting in our theater work.

Directing Approach and Method Acting

During his graduate studies at UMass, Clark became familiar with various acting approaches, including the work of Stanislavski, Augusto Boal, Lee Strasberg, Tyrone Guthrie, Joseph Papp, Stella Adler, Uta Hagen, Kristin Linklater, Anne Bogart, Robert Wilson, and Richard Foreman. He was grounded in theory and performance studies, while I was theatrically illiterate. But I was intuitive, loved drama and literature, and had studied Method acting. This impressed Clark much more than it should have, since at the time I was married to an aspiring actor (we had moved to Hollywood so he could find roles while I took classes).

Method acting is the American derivative of the Moscow (Russia) Art Theatre's Stanislavski method. It introduced naturalistic, emotionally honest character creation within the reality of a play. This contrasted with the then-popular demonstrative performances directed at the audience: star actors were the primary draw, and characters were "types," such as villains, unfaithful wives, dishonest merchants, etc. In the early twentieth century, Stanislavski introduced interior reality to acting at a time when literature was reflecting a parallel approach as seen in the "stream of consciousness" works by James Joyce, Virginia Woolf, and William Faulkner. The Stanislavski method also employed unity of character, time, place, and culture through vibrant directing, resulting in masterful performances.

Stanislavski brought theater into the twentieth century with systematic emphasis on the value, study and results of this work. Actors who studied the method transcended their time to communicate an emotional reality. Strasberg's training influenced my acting and directing tremendously. At twenty-one, after studying with Henry Thomas, I moved to Hollywood with my actor husband and enrolled in the Strasberg Institute. Our class of six sat onstage in a circle, practicing relaxation. The instructor, a protégé of Lee's, ensured the students were fully relaxed by approaching us in our chairs and lifting and dropping our limbs. We were required to be as pliable as rag dolls. Walking behind each person, he gently pushed each forehead back with his free hand cupped and ready to receive our dropped heads. Following relaxation, we began sensory exercises. Assignments such as "sauna," "moving through mud," or "freezing cold" could last for forty minutes of silent, individual actor work. Comprehensive sensory work was implicit in the scene exercises that followed. I did well with the sensory task to suffer from the flu. Tissues spilled from the pockets of my bathrobe, and I blew my nose at the worst times. I played that I was on my way to bed and increasingly annoyed by delays. I learned the freedom of intention, and how little words matter when compared to physical and emotional clarity.

As an actor, I prepared physically and emotionally before performances. I studied character relationships through patterns of behavior or as suggested by the script or director. As a director, I prepared for casting calls by understanding character motivation, personality quirks, unspoken tensions between people, and hidden agendas. Clark and I would adapt subtext analysis as an essential part of precasting work. I'd enter the audition with a fully formed vision of what I wanted to achieve artistically. What I did not have was a preconception of how the actor might approach the goals assigned to the character.

Actors find their characters by relying on their own personal experiences, or "sensory recall," to fulfill script demands. For example, if the script required the actor to grieve the death of a pet, he might prepare by finding some equivalent loss in his experience to match the intensity of the scene. Method philosophy was integral to Clark's and my artistic work. In acting, this includes a solid, consistent sense of character and ability to listen to others. From careful listening, authentic response follows. Planned responses are never in the moment. Actors need to know the script so well it becomes second nature. If an actor forgets his lines, remaining in character will bring him back to the storyline. Paraphrasing will cue actors back on task. The goal of good theater is to tell the story of what it is to be human, and, if well done, audience members will recognize themselves in the characters' greatness and shortcomings. A few dropped lines will remain undetected when the storyline flows.

The benefit of live theater is the unrepeatable freshness of each performance. Therefore, complete engagement is required for each rehearsal. There are no "walkthroughs" or conserving energy for opening night. Rehearsal is a process of collaboration and creation. It is in synergy that the piece forms and evolves with full participation. Marginally engaged actors disrespect their fellow artists. There are approaches I routinely use to bring actors into the world of the play. One is age regression. Once an actor knows who his or her character is, we travel back to that individual's childhood. The actor invents the character's past. As a child, was the person cherished or abandoned? Liked by his peers or rejected? What sort of student and friend was this character? How does the character currently handle disappointment? Actors invent life-changing moments that influence the character's outlook.

Every actor will invent his or her own Willie Loman (*Death of a Salesman*) or Blanche Dubois (*A Streetcar Named Desire*). He or she will develop characters based on innate personality, experience, temperament, energy, and talent. These particulars are not important for an audience to know. It is raw material the actor draws on to provide depth to the performance. It is the director's job to maximize actor attributes in the service of the production. This is done by paying careful attention to the actor's impulses, strengths, hesitations, fears, and level of risk taking and by creating a safe environment in which to challenge limitations.

One of the biggest mistakes directors and actors may make is not acknowledging the "continuous reality" of a play. When we willingly surrender disbelief, we agree to pretend the actors on stage are actual people participating in the events that are occurring. Every script covers a specific time, which is, in proportion to the overall life of the characters, a sliver. There are exceptions, but most playwrights do not try to dramatize a lifespan. In the frozen frame of time of a play, characters remain a particular age. As specific events occur, they react in alignment with their history, fears, and loves. The more comprehensively actors create a past for their characters, the richer the backstory becomes and the more levels the actor has to draw from. In addition, every spoken line and every physical move originates from need. Communication occurs for a specific purpose—to sound smart, earn praise or validation, teach, correct, or argue. Whatever the intention, it must be clear to the audience. If it appears unclear in rehearsal, it is because the actor does not know the meaning of the line or why his or her character is saying it. When a director hears a "read" line, he or she stops immediately, talks about what the characters want from each other in that moment, and sometimes has the actors improvise to establish a sense of scene dynamics. This approach operated throughout every venue of theater in which we worked. Actors must know what they want and say so with intention or their audience will not understand.

Stage design and character movement (blocking) flow from character creation and relationships with others. It is essential to know with whom the characters naturally align before directing them to stand or sit in a certain place. As a director, I watch where they instinctively move and then set blocking accordingly. It may take me several weeks to block a show because I prefer to work organically. I ask actors not to memorize their lines until we complete character exploration. Memorized lines lock intonation and limit response. The first three weeks of my rehearsals are experimental. Some actors are terribly uncomfortable with this way of working, as it is unconventional and challenging. Universal blocking symbols—d/l is shorthand for downstage left—serves as shorthand for actor movement and is oriented from the actor's point of view as he or she faces the audience. It is essential that directors, actors, and stage managers annotate scripts in this common language because blocking— once it is set—communicates relationship alliances, conflict, discomfort, and all nonverbal messages, which will be read unconsciously by the audience.

To help me imagine configurations in space and how different characters might relate to them, Clark would work on the set design as I researched the background of the script. As we made final assessments about the appropriateness of the script, Clark would put the final touches on the preliminary set, either a three dimensional model or a computer generated design.

Kathy Keena and Clark Bowlen in Stratford, Ontario.

Production Principles

Selecting a particular play is a commitment. The script must be relevant—
to us, and to our audience. We were fortunate because the college allowed
us to draw from classic and contemporary works, which a for-profit
theater company might not have been able to mount. Our productions
required a strong storyline, the evolution of characters, showing rather
than telling, and unity of time, place, and action. We carried these
principles into our later work. Our theatrical beginnings established a
pattern to which Clark and I always preferred to return.

Practical considerations, such as budget limitations and theater
constraints, are important. The size, experience, and opportunity for
casting opportunities must be fair. For example, an all-male cast was
biased against female actresses. Although such a play was not out of the
question, the college setting meant that we'd balance it with a reasonable
amount of women's theater. Recognizing the inherent racial and cultural
biases of English and American scripts, we committed ourselves to
colorblind casting, giving actors of all cultural backgrounds an equal
opportunity to play all roles. This practice also facilitated a dynamic
theatrical experience.

Within an academic setting, expectations need to be realistic. Participants may be training to become actors or merely taking an elective, and many students have little or no experience onstage. The benefit of dealing with novice actors is the absence of competition for star status, playing to the audience, or overacting. Clark and I established a collaborative atmosphere in which all participants were artists in training. Student actors had priority, but community actors were cast when students could not be found. This strengthened the shows by adding professionalism to the group.

Actors enjoy recognition from peers and community. Performance is a self-esteem booster that can be taken into management roles, public speaking, business leadership, and politics. Vocal training, breath control, and posture training enhance poise. Actors learn to channel emotion and manage feelings.

A successful production is a cathartic experience for audience and actors alike. It moves us through a compressed time in which events shift and lives permanently alter. The ending brings a newly ordered universe. In Shakespeare's day, the righteous kingdom was restored. In contemporary scripts, that new order may be a wasteland of disassociation.

CHAPTER 1

ACADEMIC THEATER, 1988 TO 1991

Clark and I met in the Humanities Department at MCC; we were colleagues who joined the faculty in 1988. We quickly discovered compatible theater interests and values and formed an alliance. We were especially suited to work together. Clark was a visual artist and set and lighting designer who saw a stable stage picture. His stunning designs enhanced the emotional composition of our productions. For me, the stage was in perpetual flux with energy combinations generated by relationships. Our combination of static and transient energies balanced our shows.

Academic theater gave us the luxury of selecting the show and the manner of development and production. The more invested the students became, the more empowered they felt. Our department attracted tremendously talented students, some of whom suffered from learning disabilities in reading and writing but could access character emotions effortlessly. A safe, supportive environment silences the inner critic and releases the free spirit.

In our early years, Clark emphasized that he was committed to developing a strong theater program for the college and establishing its reputation as a respected program. Initially, he taught acting and production classes during the day, then returned to the college to direct in the evening. After our first collaboration, I took over directing, and he was free to produce, design, teach, and promote the program.

From the start, Clark and I discussed all the scripts we wanted to direct. We both loved literature and challenged each other by questioning the patterns of various playwrights. Clark was interested in Eugene O'Neill's writing. Since 1989 marked the hundredth anniversary of O'Neill's birth, Clark said if I agreed to be the dramaturge for *Desire Under the Elms* and play the role of Abbie, he would direct and produce it in fall of 1988. After that first collaboration, I directed works by two contemporary American playwrights—Tennessee Williams and Sam Shepard—as well as one Shakespeare production, while he designed and produced.

Institutions of higher education have advantages in that they provide stability that other venue types do not guarantee. Participants pay for theater classes. For the director, this system is a privilege. Attendance is mandatory, which means the actors show up on time, ready to work. They learn blocking and lines in the time period requested. They complete the requirements for actor preparation. Since students are earning college credit, attrition is low. Dropouts usually occur at the start of the semester.

Students in production classes provide technical support, managing publicity, assembling props and costumes, building sets, running lights, etc., taking the pressure off the director and actors. Other than brief meetings with technical people for costume fittings and to try new set pieces, and a tech rehearsal to blend lights and sound with the play, the actors and director are free to focus on content. Our rehearsals were three hours long, four nights a week for ten weeks of a twelve-week semester.

Academic theater provides a budget for modest productions of contemporary and classical shows. For us, it was $3,000 per production, from which the director was paid $1,000. Although as an instructor at the college, I could triple that teaching a course, the community rate for directing a show was $1,000. If you work in the theater, however, money is not your motivation. In addition, the college supported our productions with a community weekend featuring seminars, workshops, and a discussion following the play. The house filled, and English classes wrote production reviews. The campus and local newspapers also covered the shows. We were in the fortunate position of developing and nurturing potential actors.

1988: *Desire Under the Elms* by Eugene O'Neill

Background

An inexorable fatalism runs through Eugene O'Neill's plays of passion and betrayal—a combination of his personality, education, and experience. His models include Greek tragedy and Elizabethan drama, in which people are born under certain stars and therefore are predetermined to follow a certain course of events. O'Neill also inherited the judgmental attitude of Puritanism, which is the backdrop of his play *Desire Under the Elms.*

O'Neill was born into an unusual family. His father, James O'Neill, was a Shakespearian actor who made his fortune playing the lead in *The Count of Monte Cristo,* a popular melodrama of the day, sacrificing his classical stage career in the process. An Irish immigrant, James was terrified of poverty. Ella, his wife, was much younger than James and star struck. However, she was not prepared for a life of stage touring and fared poorly as a mother. Their first child, Jamie, was five years old when she gave birth to her second, Edmund, who lived only one year. Ella was touring with James and the children were being cared for elsewhere, when Jamie contracted measles; baby Edmund caught them and died. Jamie was sent away to school immediately. Third child Eugene was born ten years after Jamie, and according to family lore, the difficult pregnancy resulted in Ella's addiction to morphine. James apparently chose the doctor, who prescribed morphine as an alternative to in-patient treatment. It is difficult to know whether James was negligent; at the time, morphine was legal. What is clear is that Eugene blamed his father for his mother's addiction. In O'Neill's autobiographical *Long Day's Journey into Night,* the father is repeatedly accused of being miserly. The truth is, the O'Neill family was riddled with addiction. James was a hard-drinking man who nevertheless remained the family wage earner for fifty years. Son Jamie was a full-fledged alcoholic by age twenty and met an early death. Eugene was well on his way to alcoholism but was able to discontinue drinking as he achieved success as a writer.

Synopsis

Desire Under the Elms was written in 1924, a third of the way through O'Neill's writing career, which began in 1913 and ended in 1943. The story is of an aging farmer, Ephraim, farming on near barren New Hampshire soil. Two previous wives have died, presumably due to the harsh conditions. Ephraim has three grown sons who help manage the farm. The eldest two, from the first marriage, decide to leave after learning their father has gone to town to take a new wife. There are multiple allusions to Ephraim as miserly and heartless. Youngest son, twenty-five, falls in love with thirty-five-year-old bride, a loving, passionate woman who wants a home but clearly has no interest in her elderly husband. She becomes pregnant with his child, telling Ephraim the boy is his son. But the birth has complicated family life, since Ephraim announces the farm will go his young wife and the baby. The young man reveals the true paternity of the child and tells his lover he wishes the baby had never been born. Desperate to retain his love, she commits infanticide. This dooms her to pay for her crime, implied to be death. Before she goes to her sentence, however, her lost lover returns to tell her he will share the punishment with her.

This is an absolute American morality play based on flawed redemption where sins cannot be forgiven. O'Neill's posthumous *Long Day's Journey into Night* contains many of the same elements:

1. A miserly older father with unrealistic expectations of himself replays his youth to the disapproval of those around him,
2. An ingénue wife does some incredibly stupid things, finally engulfing and destroying the final vestiges of family for all,
3. The youngest son, a romantic, restless and seeking redemption, with self-serving sibling(s) is hopelessly attached to mother/lover figure,
4. A dead baby.

As in all good tragedy, events overtake the characters, and they become victims of circumstance. As consequences overtake individuals, events trigger further events that lead to catastrophic outcomes. In this case, Abbie's panic that she might lose Eben's love causes her to kill her baby, hoping to return to her life before the baby's birth. Her tragic flaw—loving Eben too much and the baby too little—kills her. Eben and Abbie's belief that their secret love will remain undiscovered is delusional and tragic, as is Ephraim's dream to raise yet a third family with a third wife at age seventy-five. Yet he would rather set the farm on fire than pass it on to anyone he feels does not deserve it. In the end, O'Neill's characters are abandoning and abandoned. There is some consolation in that Abbie and Eben have each other until death, but this is small. The drama is strongly Judeo-Christian with ample doses of damnation. My artistic conclusion was that O'Neill wanted to purge his demons by telling the story of a selfish father; a frustrated, mismatched younger wife; the sons who were casualties of this union; and the ensuing mistakes they made as they repeatedly failed to understand one another and climbed deeper into isolation.

Challenges

As director, Clark emphasized the play was about the ownership of a farm. Everyone had his or her own reasons for wanting the farm, each in competition against the others. The farm had been barren, with people as unyielding as the soil. Ephraim persevered to make it work, but it also made him hard. His sons lived without the softness of their mother. The house had serviceable edges but lacked warmth. Always operative was the Puritan work ethic that labor is it is own reward, and mankind is born into sinfulness and easily misguided.

Clark's sets were clean, understated designs that furthered the storyline of the play. They promoted symbolic comprehension. Instead of a closed structure for the first floor, Clark designed "open walled" rooms suggested only by frames. This allowed audience to see through the house with an omniscient viewpoint, further heightening the triangulation of the relationships. He designed a storage cabinet, which functioned as part of the furniture, and housed lighting instruments. These created stunning elm tree patterns on the interior during night scenes and also seemed to embrace the house like arms.

Every semester resulted in a production presented to the larger campus. It usually coincided with an Arts Weekend during which students participated in post show discussion with the actors. This validated the students' experience, emphasizing their significance in the creation of the performance.

Actors

Desire Under the Elms is the only play in this collection I did not direct. Yet I had a role in the conception and production and as the dramaturge. I also played Abbie, the character who propelled the action of the play, and therefore can discuss issues common among the cast.

One essential requirement for all actors is to believe the environment is a harsh, cruel place, unwelcoming to life. Everything is stunted: Ephraim's sons are deprived of a mother; Ephraim is deprived of a loving partner. Everything is scarce, with too little farm yield and too few hands to complete the grueling work. Deprivation is both physical and emotional. It is impossible to know if the land turned Ephraim into a hard-hearted man or if he came to the rocky land with a hard heart. Abbie enters this environment as a soft, sensual female, someone who is not emotionally shut down. At every turn, she is thwarted by rejection and coldness. The only humane person she encounters is Eben, the youngest and most malleable member of the family. Their passion will work only if the tension of a punishing environment is successfully conveyed, and each character projects an unfulfilled longing. Abbie is just a step away from desperation. She has married an old man she does not love. If it is property or money she wants, she has made a terrible choice. At the most, she will inherit a broken-down farm in the middle of nowhere, that is, if she's lucky and successfully fights his sons. As she gradually recognizes the utter bleakness of her circumstances, she impulsively reaches for the forbidden. If we look at this as a morality play, we see the world is cold and harsh; anyone who does not accept this reality will be punished by death. Thus the pace should be inexorable.

Abbie (Kathleen Keena) watches Eben (Neil Rittenband) as her husband
Ephraim (Ted Wholsen) sleeps. Set and lighting design by Clark Bowlen.

Eben (Neil Rittenband) listens as Abbie (Kathleen Keena) tries to
influence him. Set and lighting design by Clark Bowlen.

Abbie (Kathleen Keena) collapses under the stern words of Ephraim
(Ted Wholsen). Set and lighting design by Clark Bowlen.

1989: *The Glass Menagerie* by Tennessee Williams

Background

Following *Desire*, Clark invited me to direct a show of my choice. I selected *The Glass Menagerie* by Tennessee Williams more from instinct than literary assessment. The poignant story of family on the brink of an essential shift held great appeal for me. The moment between actualization and total annihilation, inherently dramatic, is present in everyday circumstances, although not as distinctively as in this script. William's skill in condensing a critical juncture in one monumental evening expresses the brevity and enormity in which such events occur. Clark concurred it was a great play for my premiere as a college director.

Williams is considered by many to be American's premiere playwright, second only to O'Neill. He is known for *A Streetcar Named Desire*, whose original production starred Marlon Brando as Stanley. Like O'Neill's *Desire Under the Elms*, *The Glass Menagerie* is based on William's childhood. His sister, Rose, who began suffering from mental illness at age fourteen and underwent a lobotomy as a young adult, is a central figure. Brother and sister were extremely close as children. Amanda, their mother, is the overly anxious, controlling damsel of southern plantation life, who has been left to raise her children alone—the archetypical Williams character. The absent father, who in real life came and went, is an alcoholic shoe salesman. (Williams claimed the domineering character of Big Daddy in *Cat on a Hot Tin Roof* was based on his father.) The narrator of the play, who first appears on stage "dressed as a merchant sailor" is Williams, who served for a time as a merchant marine. Tennessee Williams's works are infused with fragile Southern belles, crumbling plantations, inarticulate males, sexual ambiguity, and a lyrical quality with a remorseful tone.

Synopsis

The script can be easily misinterpreted as Laura's love story, since she is introduced to her potential suitor in the final act, or as Amanda's play as she attempts to launch Laura into respectable adult life. But William's production notes are quite clear: this is a memory play, and in memory, the picture is "a more penetrating and vivid expression of things as they are." The question is, whose memory? The answer must be Tom's. If there is any doubt, Williams dispels it with his use of backlit projections, both images and titles, to illustrate the action. These include titles such as "This is my sister: celebrate her with strings!" and images of a high-school hero and other visual aids to dramatize the story. Williams purposefully highlights specific points, while admitting his memory has manufactured distortions. Tom's character mentions the social background of the play, which he describes as "the huge middle class of America matriculating in a school for the blind … having their fingers pressed forcibly down on the fiery Braille alphabet of a dissolving economy." There is specific music designated for Laura's interaction with the glass menagerie to sound like "inexpressible sorrow." The musical fragments recur, like memory, and are never complete. There is also 1930s music from the dance hall that is heard on the apartment fire escape.

In addition to projections and music, Williams suggests that the lighting be "the atmosphere of memory, the stage is dim. Shafts of light are focused on selected areas or actors, sometimes in contradistinction to what is the apparent center." For Laura, he suggests "a peculiar pristine clarity such as light used in early religious portraits of female saints or madonnas." The fact that the play is a memory, and that Tom is outside the set while he introduces the play and only enters the set afterward, informs our production. That he is dressed as a merchant marine and prepared to become a character emphasizes his self-consciousness. It is as if he is underscoring the presentational aspects to explain to his audience:

> You can never understand how insufferable my life in Saint Louis was unless you lived it. You will never understand how unable our mother was to provide for us or how unsuited my sister was for adult life. You will never know how everything creative in me was dying by continuing to support them. Unlike my father, I carry the burden of my abandonment with me eternally. If he had been responsible for the family, I would never have been asked to shoulder this. Let me show you how it was.

The play then dramatizes the family's preparation for the event that changed their lives forever. A high-school friend who works with Tom is invited to the house as a possible match for Laura. Improbably, but wonderfully, it is the boy on whom Laura had a crush in school. He is gentle, kind, and loving to her. She shows him her treasured glass collection, her private interior world. But whatever connection they have ends abruptly when he reveals that he is engaged. We are left with the disturbing reality that neither Laura nor Amanda will be able to take care of themselves, and Tom won't be able to do so either.

Challenges

Clark designed a World War II cargo ship as the setting where the memory is revealed. The Wingfields' apartment was on top of the ship's gray deck. Upstage center, a projection screen displayed slides reflecting either the emotional or historical content of the narration. In front of the screen was the dining area. Downstage center was the living room; downstage left, the glass collection. Stage right was the fire escape/ship's bow from which Tom begins his narration. For its originality and execution, Clark's set received the prestigious Ming Cho Lee Award in the American College Theater Festival (ACTF). The blurring of generational and familial boundaries is a theme of the play; magic, light and crystal, and freshness and decay are also prominent motifs. Twenty-one-year-old Tom takes on the role of wage earner and caretaker for the household due to an absent father. His mother dresses in her girlhood frock and flirts with twenty-three-year-old Jim, Tom's friend from the warehouse. The brother and sister's relationship recalls lost, romantic love, and William's production notes cast Laura in Madonna-like lighting, certainly implying virginal mystery. When Jim dances with Laura and accidentally breaks her glass unicorn's horn, it becomes just like the other unicorns. This is a symbolic taking of Laura's uniqueness, broken by Jim's appearance. The actors used these sexual overtones as subtext, and their body language worked well with the dialogue. In Tom's drunken scene, for example, when Laura must let him into the locked apartment, I directed the actor to bring Laura the gift of a scarf, which he tries unsuccessfully to put around her shoulders before passing out, thus symbolizing his unsuccessful attempt to possess her sexually. I interpreted Tom's retelling of the story as his eternal link to her, which he will replay throughout his life.

Actors

Ensemble work was a vital part of our rehearsal process. Actors improvised various configurations of brother/sister, mother/sister, mother/brother, brother/friend, and sister/friend to determine interdependencies and resentments. Tom's sarcasm with his mother, his tenderness with his sister, Amanda's hysterical dramatization, and Laura's counterbalancing passivity were developed individually and in relationship with other cast members. Alliances, especially brother and sister, were emphasized. I also gave the actors playing Laura and Tom the motivation of unacknowledged incestuous attraction in addition to their attachment to each other.

Clark Bowlen's 3-D model for *The Glass Menagerie* set design.

Tom (Tim Protzman), standing outside the production on the deck of a cargo ship, introduces the story. Set and lighting design by Clark Bowlen.

Laura (Ross Nass) is bathed in Madonna-like light as she gazes at her glass collection. Set and lighting design by Clark Bowlen.

Laura (Rose Nass) and Amanda (Marcia Jean) are dressed in their finest for the gentleman caller. Note the projected image that conveys the emotional essence of the moment. Set and lighting design by Clark Bowlen.

1990: *Buried Child* by Sam Shepard

Background

With the success of *The Glass Menagerie*, including Clark's award-winning design, the department was earning a solid reputation. Clark told me I was the better director and that he hoped I would direct future shows. Since I preferred directing to acting, coaching, researching or advising, I was energized. He suggested that we focus next contemporary American playwright Sam Shepard, a descendant of O'Neill and Williams, but bleaker. Unlike O'Neill's and Williams's plays, Shepard's works do not have a spiritual redemption that transcends tragedy (e.g., O'Neill's lovers) or eternal passion that animates life (e.g., Tom's love for Rose).

Clark recommended giving students of all races and cultures equal opportunities to audition. *Buried Child* became our first production to feature colorblind casting, which made the plays more powerful due to the implicit message of universality. *Buried Child* is less popular than Shepard's other plays, although not inferior in quality. It is perhaps less accessible because of its somewhat macabre elements—fallow ground yields a fantastic crop of vegetables and then the corpse of a baby. I, much more than Clark, preferred dark plays of secret intrigue, because I found them more of a directing challenge.

Born in Illinois, Shepard writes about western Americana where wide-open spaces separate residences and mirror the vacancy of familial connection. Roaming his plays are a collection of people who do not know where their homes are, were, or could be. Those who traditionally have the answers—mothers, fathers, brothers, sisters, partners, and clergy—are inherently clueless about one another's needs and desires. There is no collective memory of a better day. Their common denominator is rootlessness. When people say they will be back shortly, they often go for days and may come back in unpredictable states of agitation or crisis.

Shepard's scripts might be described as postapocalyptic; they are marked by individual disengagement and filled with wounded people. He is author of *A Lie of the Mind*, *Curse of the Starving Class*, *Fool for Love*, *Savage Love*, and *True West*, among numerous others. Although dead bodies litter Shepard's stage, no one grieves. The Pulitzer Prize–winning *Buried*

Child is aptly named. Not only is the family secret about a drowned baby, but the case may be made that Dodge, Tilden, Bradley, and Vince are buried children. These four men, spanning three generations, are unable to relate to each other. Although grandson Vince recognizes his father Tilden and grandfather Dodge, they don't remember him. Meanwhile Dodge's wife is preoccupied with commemorating their deceased son Ansel with "a big, tall statue with a basketball in one hand and a rifle in the other." These two symbols of masculinity, combined as a shrine for a dead youth, are eminently absurd.

Synopsis

Dodge, in his seventies when the play opens, is a long-time alcoholic in his final days. His only company is the TV screen. His wife can be heard upstairs, talking "at" him, oblivious to his sarcasm. She is self-absorbed and eager to appear the perfect Christian. She insists she won't be long, yet is gone for most of the ensuing action. Son Tilden is charged with watching Dodge, but steals his father's alcohol as soon as his mother leaves. Tilden, earlier presumed to be living independently in New Mexico, is mentally handicapped. He has lately returned to his parents' home due to unbearable loneliness. A torrential rainstorm in the backyard has yielded a crop of corn, although the land has been fallow since 1935, which Tilden harvests, then dumps in Dodge's lap. Tilden (the tiller of soil) continues to bring in crops from the backyard throughout the play. Something strange is happening to the house and its inhabitants.

I suggested to Clark that Shepard might be using the metaphor of landscape dominance to suggest de-humanization. We discussed the possibility of outside growth making its way into the house between the floorboards, winding around staircases and dangling from ceilings. I wanted to work with the concept of a reverse Eden, where primitive forces overtaking manmade order. Although not as overtly absurd as Eugene Ionesco's *Rhinoceros*, *Buried Child* does contain elements of the outrageous.

During the rainstorm, Bradley, the younger son who "chopped off his leg with a chain saw," according to Halie, enters the house while Dodge sleeps. Still violent, Bradley hacks off Dodge's hair, leaving his head bleeding. Violence is repeated with Shelley, grandson Vince's girlfriend, when Bradley forces her mouth open so that he can insert three fingers in a symbolic rape. People are motivated by revenge and cruelty toward family and strangers alike in a heartless universe. Dodge, however, committed the initial violence, more than thirty years ago, when his wife delivered a baby he had not fathered: he drowned the child. He continues "to dodge" this family secret, although it has effectively destroyed the family functioning. He does refer to a time when they were a "well-established family ... pointed toward what looked like the middle part of our life." Grandson Vince has been away from home for six years. He returns to find that his grandfather and his father do not recognize him.

Three generations of men feel displaced in their families. Dodge feels like a stranger in his marriage, tells his son Tilden to leave, and denies he has a grandchild. Tilden cannot remember his son Vince, yet he is haunted by the memory of his dead brother, whom he used to care for. Vince remembers his family, but although he is eager to reconnect, his father is incapable of doing so. Bradley is disowned by his father and terrorizes his brother. No one is able to welcome or console anyone else. Family members traumatize Vince's girlfriend, who stays at the house while Vince goes out. Vince returns outrageously drunk and acts the part of a soldier attacking enemy territory using empty bottles as bombs. Father Dewis (do less) is utterly amoral and without ability to judge good or evil. Vince cuts through the screen porch like a commando with a knife in his teeth. Dodge announces his death is imminent and wills the house to Vince (invincible), who announces he must stay to set things right. He describes seeing his face in the windshield change into his father's, his grandfather's, and "his whole race behind him" until everything dissolves. He assumes Dodge's position on the couch, leaving open to speculation whether he will truly turn anything around or become the next in the long line of self-destructive men. He is alone in a house where no one has recognized him, his girlfriend has left him, and his father is carrying the corpse of a baby up the stairs to his grandmother, while his grandfather lies dead on the floor.

Challenges

The power of nature overtaking the house was symbolically significant to me, and I emphasized this component as Clark developed the set. I regarded the rampant vegetable growth as the substitution for neglected family growth, which caused the primitive to overtake the human. Primitive, inhumane behaviors are buried in the backyard, but surface again as nature uncovers that which man seeks to hide. Due to this buried secret, the family unit becomes a collection of strangers. To illustrate this hopelessness, we opened the show with the song "Riders of the Storm" by the Doors. It has the wonderful thunder and Jim Morrison's death-in-life voice singing, "Into this house we're born, into this world we're thrown. Like a dog without a bone, an actor out alone, riders on the storm." We used other music by the Doors, including "People are Strange" and "Just One More Kiss," a deathly vacuous song of disturbing alienation. The set contained a broken-down couch, dilapidated staircase, and crumbling downstairs occupied by an alcoholic—a private hell. Clark's spectacular lighting—photographs show the gradual passing of night and the unearthly beginning of a new dawn—was apocalyptically beautiful. The primal, even prehistoric light suggested backward time travel.

Actors

When working with the actors, I used Dodge's decomposition as a starting point. Before Halie became pregnant with another man's child, he says, their family was respectable. According to Dodge, his wife's infidelity is unforgivable. Whatever they did have together is now irredeemably lost. Halie is a superficial social climber who is trying to ingratiate herself with a particularly ignorant priest. She speaks at Dodge rather than to him, as an object rather than a person. In turn, fueled by resentment, he creates a caricature out of her. This energy of mutual disrespect and blame permeates the house. A powerless Dodge and his manipulative spouse are loosely held together by some forgotten agreement. The house's inhabitants are numb with ignored pain and unacknowledged disappointment. Whoever enters this environment is affected and transformed by the energy in some way— different for each individual, but hurtful to all. They are all characters searching for connection and home, but none are satisfied. They remain strangers. The task for each actor is to recognize his or her character's search for recognition and how the inability to find it diminishes life. The resulting violence, addiction, lack of empathy, and desertion all evolve from this disconnection with others.

Clark Bowlen's set model for *Buried Child*.

Daytime: Vince (Craig Kennedy Johnston) steals Bradley's wooden leg as Shelley (Kelli Bailey) approaches from the backyard. Lighting and set design by Clark Bowlen.

Nighttime: Bradley (Tim Lagosh) sleeps as Shelley (Kelli Bailey) waits for Vince to return. Note the change in lighting from the previous photograph. Lighting and set design by Clark Bowlen.

Tilden (Sam Winston) cradles the corpse of the drowned baby after retrieving it from the grave in the backyard while Vince (Craig Kennedy Johnston) sleeps. Lighting and set design by Clark Bowlen.

Dodge (R. T. Donnelly) is slumped on the floor, unconscious.
Lighting and set design by Clark Bowlen.

1991: *The Taming of the Shrew* by William Shakespeare

Background

Clark and I would travel by train to New York City to attend premieres of directors such as Anne Bogart or Robert Wilson, actors like Kathleen Turner and Al Pacino, or a show given a favorable review in *American Theater*. We frequently traveled to Massachusetts—to Cambridge to see ART (American Repertory Theater) and to Williamstown, where we saw an unforgettable *Mother Courage* starring Olympia Dukakis. We were regulars at Yale Repertory and Long Wharf in New Haven, Connecticut, and Hartford Stage and TheaterWorks in Hartford, Connecticut.

But by far our most valuable and influential theater experience was our annual trip to the Shakespeare Festival in Stratford, Ontario. Founded in summer of 1953 by Tyrone Guthrie, Stratford was an internationally acclaimed repertory company specializing in Shakespeare and attracted distinguished stage actors. From its first four seasons in a tent, the company had blossomed into a main stage modeled after London's Globe, where Shakespeare was part-owner and his plays were performed. In addition to the Festival Theatre's spectacular three-quarter, all-wood thrust stage on two diagonals with interior entrances, exits, and a working balcony with staircase, there were three other theaters—the Avon, the Tom Patterson, and the Studio. The four theatres were designed in different configurations to facilitate various types of performance. The Festival Theatre's capacity is 1,826 seats; the Avon, 1,090 seats; the Patterson, 480; and the Studio, 260.

The town entirely accommodates itself to the repertory season, with residents opening their homes to theatergoers as bed and breakfasts, and the theater business office arranging reservations with the purchase of tickets. The season begins in late spring and runs through fall. The company truly works in repertory. One can see actors in leading roles one night and in supporting roles at a matinee the next afternoon. The plays are formidable and include the entire collection of Shakespeare; Greek tragedy and comedy; Restoration drama; and works by internationally renowned playwrights such as Albee, Beckett, Brecht, Chekhov, Hellman, Ibsen, O'Casey, Miller, Wilde, Williams, and promising new Canadian writers. Stratford also produces, quite elaborately and usually on the main stage, musicals such as *Fiddler on the Roof*, *A Funny Thing Happened on the Way to the Forum*, *Guys and Dolls*, *Gypsy*, *My Fair Lady*, and *Oliver*, to name a few.

Clark and I were profoundly influenced by the work done at Stratford. For classical theater, little set dressing was used beyond world-class costuming, lighting, and sound. The spacious stage allowed the actors to work different areas to symbolize different physical regions, war camps, or government palaces. Sometimes one object would be soundlessly dropped into a scene to establish a sense of place, disappearing before the next scene. From this we realized how little scenery and crowded sets were needed to create drama. Clear elocution was a high priority for Stratford actors, as is needed by Shakespeare's plays, which have such visually rich description. The tremendous discipline required of a Shakespearian actor translates into sophisticated training for any performer. Many famous TV and film actors performed at Stratford before moving on to the work on the screen. Examples include Michael Caine, Lorne Greene, Julie Harris, James Mason, William Shatner, and Jessica Tandy. Others—such as Brian Bedford, James Blendick, Peter Donaldson, Colm Feore, Martha Henry, William Hutt, Diane Leblanc, Seana McKenna, William Needles, Stephen Ouimette, Lucy Peacock, Nicholas Pennell, Christopher Plummer, and Maggie Smith have made their careers as lifetime repertory company members.

By 1991, Clark and I were talking about how we could produce nontraditional Shakespeare, as Stratford sometimes did, by costuming actors in another time period, in contemporary clothing, or in clothing related to a certain group of people. One problem at a community college is the constant shift of the actor pool. We knew it would take two semesters to train students to perform Shakespeare and learn the difficult parts succinctly, developing character and the natural movement required to make the production work. However, our joint enthusiasm overcame our considerations, and soon we were discussing our first Shakespeare venture. Clark and I agreed that it ought to be a comedy, which would be more accessible to students and audience than a tragedy. We felt *The Taming of the Shrew* translated best to the contemporary stage, because the power struggle between genders has timeless appeal.

Clark saw beyond the college and imagined that we might tour the show as an independent theater company. Shakespeare Hartford was born. The Hartford Downtown Council agreed that our company could perform at historic sites downtown at lunchtime. Our proposal recommended a financial arrangement with Tim Proxman's Merriment and Mystery Productions Company to cover the rental of an outdoor sound system, its operator, and costumes. Originally, I wanted Petruchio to ride a motorcycle center stage, making an impressive rock star entrance and looking like Jim Morrison. We received approval from the council in the summer and proceeded to plan our first street theater Shakespeare.

Synopsis

The artistic concept was to contemporize the show into a rock version, with Petruchio, à la Jim Morrison, rock-star sexy in leather. Unlike other men who run in the opposite direction, he pursues Kate, the fiercely independent, avant-garde artist who resists convention to protect her autonomy. Her sister, Bianca, a traditional woman with mild ways and a pleasing manner, is extremely attractive to suitors. Her winning suitor, Lucentio, an Elvis Presley type, represents the kind of man whose notion of romantic love is taken from songs rather than reality. He is scheduled for a rude awakening around act 5. Our soundtrack featured music by legendary lovers John Lennon and Yoko Ono; it focused not only on female/male dynamics, but also East/West tension and the restoration of balance. Restoring order from chaos is a dominant theme in Shakespeare's scripts. *Shrew* has a strong theme of dissembling, and it is essential to recognize that Petruchio does not simply seek to thwart Kate. He is acting the part of a bully in order to outmaneuver her and make her aware of her own behavior, so she will no longer need to use it as protection.

Petruchio says from the outset that he loves a good chase and repeatedly demonstrates he is having a wonderful time. For example, when he chides the tailor for making an unacceptable dress for Kate, he privately insists that the tailor be paid. When Kate argues his objections are unreasonable, he is actually helping her to develop her reasonable nature. In this process, it is important to recognize that Kate begins to respect and then fall in love with Petruchio. And why not? He is entirely ready to challenge her in any argument and enjoys the struggle. They are intellectual equals. His justification that withholding food, rest, and clothing are necessary until appropriate choices are found irks Kate, who sees her own behavior in his exaggerations.

Certain issues become very difficult for the young woman. Although her mother has promised Kate will marry him as long as he wins her love, Kate appears to continue scorning her suitor. Yet she cries when Petruchio is late, clearly demonstrating her attachment. When he does appear, improperly dressed, he announces he must leave before the reception. When she begs him to stay, he insists she leave with him. Kate clearly intended to enjoy her wedding reception. Petruchio is the only man who bothers to learn how she thinks or why. He takes enjoyment in matching her verbally, challenging her, and admiring her quick wit. He praises her high-spiritedness; when she is at her most outrageous, he dares to match her with more outrageousness. In the process, he comes to know who she is.

There is no such luck for Lucentio and Bianca. Lucentio marries an ideal, not a real woman. Bianca says she will learn her lessons to please herself. She encourages Lucentio to woe her, but compliance is not the same as trust. When Lucentio bids Bianca to come to him, she "is busy and she cannot come." If she knew the husbands had placed a wager on their wives, would she care to participate? The logic of the play implies she would not.

Challenges

The Taming of the Shrew is given the "frame" of a drunkard who falls asleep and awakens to be told he is a lord and a play is awaiting his attendance. Although this device seemed too cumbersome for street theater, we did want to retain the conscious playacting spirit. To accomplish this, I had actors use oversized fans, which they alternately hid behind and revealed themselves as they made their way from the rear of the audience to the front of the stage. As they began, Yoko Ono's "Don't Be Scared" cued over the sound system, with its delicate yet slightly lunatic vocal:

Don't be scared to love.
Better to love than never love at all.
Don't be shy. Don't be shy to tell.
You may lose the chance to tell.
Don't be shy.
When your hearts are lit, use your survival kit.
Then you never have to run away.
Sun in the east, moon in the west. Both moving slow.
There's no landing sight at all, where we go.

To illustrate Petruchio's playacting the bully, and express his deepest feelings for Kate, I used "Forgive Me, My Little Flower Princess" by John Lennon, which apologizes for his brutality:

… for brushing your delicate neck,
forgive me for my selfishness,
forgive me.
I know there is no way to repay you,
for every day I will try to,
for the rest of my life I will thank you,
thank you, thank you.

Finally, to recap both positions, Yoko's "You're the One" seemed the perfect rock number:

Mountains may rise, rivers may run,
but you make me be myself.
How do I tell you? You're the one.
Stars may move, time may run,
but you make me free myself.
How do I tell you? You're the one.

John Lennon and Yoko Ono, larger-than-life, rock-star-crossed lovers, were also duplicated in all white, contemporary chic for the wedding scene.

As mentioned above, it is impossible to prepare a Shakespeare production in one semester, even with experienced actors. Shakespeare's language is dense and relies on pauses, comprehension of the action, playing the subtext, and sophisticated timing. The breath work and vocal projection alone can take a semester. We had no such luxury. We cast our show in the summer and began rehearsal during the summer break. We spent the second semester developing the characters and scene work and working with the difficult language of the play.

We also looked at many sites in Hartford, but settled on the Old State House because it was located in the well-trafficked downtown business center. Lawn seating worked well for our lunchtime audiences. Highway entrances and exits were accessible. On one of our performance days, in the spirit of festive theater, the infamous Hooker Day Parade swept past us, waving.

Actors

We continued our practice of multicultural casting, adding cross-gender casting where appropriate. Kate and Bianca's father became a mother. We modeled then mayor of Hartford, Carrie Saxon-Perry, as our Baptista, who was played masterfully by Carolyn Dixon, former director of Greater Hartford Academy of Performing Arts. Debra Walsh, an acting teacher at Greater Hartford, played Petruchio's manservant Grumio. She remained three steps ahead of the action, abruptly appearing on stage to startle audience as she reported the increasingly troubled relationship between the newlyweds. Student actors Catherine Toti and Mat Thomsen played romantic leads Kate and Petruchio. Their spirited, focused work provided a model for actors in rehearsal sessions. Bianca, played by Orlene Green, was the favored daughter, while Kate was the more difficult, rebellious child. Her parents had tried to minimize her high spiritedness, without success. Both sisters represented one half of a complete woman.

Clark and I found the size of a Shakespeare cast, generally sixteen to seventeen actors, and the logistics of performing outdoors, to be unique. As an actor, I had waited for hours in a hallway until the director called me into rehearsal for ten minutes of blocking. Both Clark and I had no interest in wasting the actors' time, and planned schedules around group scenes and other rehearsals for specific actors. Our only difficult days were during tech week, in which all cast are required to attend. Tech week was admittedly tedious for such a large cast; actors were required to be silent on the set, catch all cues, slog through two and a half hours, and retain their performance energy. Our first performances were indoors at the college. When we went outdoors, we had to deal with microphones and an outdoor sound system as well as adjusting to an entirely different performance space. It was to our benefit that we set the story in modern day Hartford with rock-and-roll costuming. This made it fun for actors and audience.

Clark strolls behind Stratford's Festival Theatre. The exterior was constructed to look like a tent.

Kathy at Stratford in the picnic area, facing the Thames River.

Baptista (Carolyn Dixon) listens to Tranio (Dave Walton) as Petruchio
(Mat Tomsen) attempts to control Kate (Catherine Toti).

Suitors Hortentio (Andrew Milliot) and Lucentio (Christopher Hartel) court Bianca (Orlene Green) while she plays it coy.

The Widow (Kerry Rohrbach) confronts Kate (Catherine Toti) as Petruchio (Mat Thomsen) tries to defend her. Curtis (Elizabeth Reynolds) and Vincentio (Dana Ring) look on helplessly.

Petruchio (Mat Thomsen) and Kate (Catherine Toti)
enjoy a moment of mutual surrender.

The entire cast from left to right: David Pryzby, Sy Levin, Samantha
Tarzia, Dave Walton, Carolyn Dixon, Orlene Green, Christopher
Hartel, Catherine Toti, Mat Thomsen, Andrew Milliot, Kerry Rohrbach,
Debra Walsh, Elizabeth Reynolds, Dana Ring, Niki Harris.

CHAPTER 2
ACADEMIC THEATER, 1992 TO 1997

From 1992 to 1997, still building the MCC theater program, we ventured into a slightly more difficult Shakespeare production, *A Midsummer Night's Dream*. Again, it was under the auspices of MCC and the Greater Hartford Downtown Council. We now knew more about producing Shakespeare, but that worked as an advantage and a detriment. We were aware of the actor preparation that was required and the staging difficulties we had to overcome. We were less naïve and recognized the limitations of our time and budget constraints. Our concept was to use script poetry in a hip-hop format, turning the forest world into city streets at night. Again, we set the story in a contemporary setting to ensure audience access, and it was our highest-attended show ever. From MCC, we toured it to the Hartford Civic Center.

During this time, we also introduced two original plays by local journalist Steve Starger. We first met Steve when he interviewed us for the *Hartford Courant*'s arts section about our hip-hop *Midsummer*. We later learned that he was an aspiring playwright and had written a one-act play, *All Sunsets Look Alike*, specifically for his actor cousin. Steve's writing is musical, graceful, and exquisite. Our next production was his play. It began an enduring artistic relationship that would span our theater career and beyond Clark's death.

Between our productions of Steve's one-act play and his full-length script, *The Man Who Knew Trotsky*, I directed and acted in *Dutchman* with my colleague Bill Foster at Naugatuck Community College; we then took that show to MCC. I discovered that simultaneous directing and acting was a risk I would not try again. The split focus guarantees the directing, acting, or both will suffer. As great as it was to be on stage as Lula, I much preferred the distance and overview required for directing. For me, it is easy, but also disturbing, to enter a character's consciousness. As a director, I can try on different characters briefly when working with actors, but I never have to commit to a specific personality.

Our last show of this period—perhaps the most daring—was our original show *Who By Fire*, featuring selected narratives from Mark Baker's *Nam: The Vietnam War in the Words of the Men and Women Who Fought There* as well as original writing by cast members who had served in Vietnam. This show subsequently toured several high schools and VA hospitals.

1992: *A Midsummer Night's Dream* by William Shakespeare

Background

A Midsummer Night's Dream was our second Shakespeare venture, and it was more challenging than *Shrew* in terms of directing and design. Clark and I were both feeling the success of our first Shakespeare undertaking and were proud we'd made it accessible to Hartford's lunchtime business crowd. The Hartford Downtown Council had provided funding, and we felt invincible, having surprised ourselves with our achievement. Clark and I were discovering we were efficient, organized leaders. Our styles were different but complementary. Clark was a meticulous planner, an artist, and a craftsman. My style was expansive, exploratory, and unexpected. He reined me in, and I gave him flying lessons. We delighted each other by discovering a middle ground that supported, without compromise, the other's style. Some students assuredly preferred Clark's leadership to mine, and vice versa. But our artistic goals remained aligned.

We selected *Midsummer* because, although it was a comedy, it was a darker, more mature work. We agreed that it was mistake to interpret the forest and fairy world as benign. Shakespeare's safety of daytime order contrasts with the mystery of the forest, where shapes, sounds, and feelings morph into unpredictable otherness. With this script, we saw the opportunity for social commentary by comparing the forest to the inner city and the safety of the city to the security of the suburbs. On a personal note, my brother John, a thirty-five-year-old career army officer, and my uncle John, retired military, had died in a private plane crash in December 1991. There was nothing I wanted to do less than direct a show. However, Clark reminded me that I'd made a commitment. I was resentful, feeling that life had broken its commitment to me. Nevertheless, I went ahead with the show, promising myself I would leave my part-time job at the college to find a professional career. My brother's life was over, and I was still hoping for a full-time job in my field. Clark never fully accepted my decision, but he respected it. He had hoped I would become a full-timer at the college but enrollment was diminishing and never did increase.

Synopsis

The play is set in ancient Athens, the birthplace of tragedy, philosophy, and Greek mythology. Shakespeare must have had felt an expansive freedom to develop the dual nature of man with poetic license. The script is filled with sleeping, dreaming, and awakening to new and surprising states of consciousness that the dreamer could not have imagined. Drugs induce love and relieve people of love sickness. Occurrences over which individuals have no control and do not understand but eventually accept are common. There is a duality to the play that suggests we are awake and asleep simultaneously, wise and foolish, divine and mortal. The audience is told that the immortal gods are fighting, and as a result

> The spring, the summer,
> The childing autumn, anger winter, change
> Their wonted liveries, and the mazed world
> By their increase now knows not which is which.
> And this same progeny of evils comes
> From our debate, from our dissension;
> We are their parents and original.

The mortals do not know why such unnatural order rules the earth. However, we can be certain that when the natural balance of affairs is out of order in Shakespeare's world, everyone suffers. An example of this disorder is Egeus emphatically insisting to the duke that his daughter Hermia marry Demetrius when she is in love with the equally appropriate Lysander. Since Egeus has no explanation for his preference, we may assume the gods' discord has compromised his judgment. The city is set up in a daytime, or rational, world of order. Social constraints and predictable mores usually guide this environment, although we know that the gods have toppled the natural order with their disagreement. In contrast to the daytime world, there is the uncharted, frightening, sexually charged forest of night, where individuals may change their shapes or voices, become suddenly enchanted by the love of an ass, fall out of love, and be betrayed by their most trusted childhood friends, deceived by their true love, or be abandoned to the dangers of wild beasts. Into this dangerous environment four young lovers enter. Their encounters are a coming-of-age story in which each faces personal fears, limitations, and misconceptions.

Challenges

To translate *Midsummer* to a contemporary setting, we chose Avon, a prestigious Hartford-area suburb, as Athens and the inner city as the forest. Our new Athens, a rational city, was a gated community of wealthy, prominent community types, removed from the dangers of drugs, guns, knives, and arson, who would meet on the golf course to discuss business and social matters. The wonderfully sultry music of Dire Straits' "My Parties" opened the golf course scene with the duke and Hippolyta, who—as in Peter Brook's 1970 production—doubled as Oberon and Titania. On the golf course, we are introduced to two rational adults who should be able to work out their differences in the light of day. The next time we meet them, they are their shadow selves—Oberon and Titania—who have quarreled over the possession of a beautiful boy for their train. Unlike Titania, Oberon has in his service a magical, trouble-loving fairy (Puck) who delights in making situations more confusing. Although Puck is confident, there is no evidence that he is effective.

Nevertheless, he brags to the other fairies that he will drug Titania, who will then fall in love with the first person she sees when she awakes.

Meanwhile, there is a parallel plot focusing on two sets of youthful lovers who have fled to the forest/street to escape the suburbs/safety as well as arranged marriages to which they do not agree. They encounter unexpected reversals of fortune, betrayals by friends, and potential threats to their lives in the dark underworld of the unconscious. Just as anything can happen in a dream, so it does to the young people, who now find themselves in a vibrant, competitive, sexual, and dangerous setting, where the unknown lurks.

Clark and I had many discussions about labeling *Midsummer* a comedy. Although it ends with the restoration of order and with marriage celebrations, the forest—street life in our production—is a threatening place from which the young lovers may not return. But it represents the necessary journey to adulthood; only by separating from the conventional rules of society do the young people become adults. The writing is in rhymed couplets, typical of Elizabethan comedy, which adds silliness to the dialogue and undercuts the threat. We both knew that traditional productions of the show portrayed the fairies as harmless, enchanting spirits. We wanted our fairies to be streetwise, threatening, armed, drug dealers. Rapping supported the concept of a risky counterculture. A third group of people also go to the forest/street to sharpen their craft. They are the Mechanicals, blue-collar workers—auto repairmen, machinists, janitors, etc.—who have formed their own group to rehearse a play for the duke and Hippolyta's wedding.

The Mechanicals give Shakespeare the opportunity to make fun of overly sensitive actors, who are too concerned about audience reaction and not worried enough about dramatic authenticity. They wonder, *What if the ladies are afraid of the lion? You better tell them you're an actor playing a lion!* They devise a prologue meant to clarify their position, but it is marred by the delivery by a company member who does not know when to end one sentence and begin the next. The actual plot of the play is the same as Romeo and Juliet, yet it is so farcically done, and with so many side comments by the audience, it is irretrievably undercut.

To design the set, Clark started with neutral white panels against a black-box theater and green turf to create the Avon golf course. Also included were a park bench and some bushes, a golf caddy, golf clubs, and daytime lighting. In the inner city forest, however, the white panels turn into a dark background of graffiti and billboards about AIDS and national brands of clothing and alcohol. Clark hung instruments to create the effect of many lit windows reflecting in the street. The inner city was the domain of the fairies or, in this case, hip-hop culture. We easily adapted the raps from Shakespeare's text, and we gave each of the fairies a solo street-dance performance. They were costumed in street chic, as were Titania and Oberon. Yet *A Midsummer Night's Dream* is no walk in the park, and it should not be staged as such. During the fearful night in the forest, when everyone has something to lose, there is little for anyone to laugh about, save Puck, who finds great delight in misinterpreting Oberon's orders. In the safety of the daylight, it is fun to laugh at the foolish lovers who, believing the other is dead, commit suicide rather than live without their love. However, how different is that from the night the lovers have just been through? Of course, it's not. If the play is to work, the terrors of the night and the unknown must remain most vivid.

Shakespeare is a master at balance. Puck urges the audience to imagine, if the play has given offense, to pretend it has all been a dream.

Actors

I called rehearsals for three different settings—the suburban scenes, the street scenes, and the mechanical scenes. At times, I felt as if I were directing three shows. By day, the duke and Hippolyta are rational adults, ruling with reason and impartiality. Yet their shadow selves, Oberon and Titania, display jealousy and adolescent behavior. Power is not shared, but clever tricks and potions are used to affect emotional states. The mature lovers' behaviors cannot be distinguished from the young lovers' foolishness. To emphasis this, we dressed Oberon and Titania in biker counterculture clothing, implying they are emotionally younger than their chronological ages. It also helped the actors physicalize their bad girl/guy alter egos. Body language in biker clothing was more aggressive, bolder, and more overtly sexual than that of reasonable suburb dwellers.

The major motivator of the young actors—whose characters must deal with sexual temptation, lack of parental oversight, and abandonment—was peer pressure and saving face. Since the student actors were actually in this life stage, it was more helpful to direct them with "you are frightened but don't want the others to know it" or "you want to be a brave male, but you are lost in the forest and want to go home." Their task was to deal with nearly total confusion and remain in control.

The fairies provide a chorus to the main story by infusing the night atmosphere with emotional undercurrents. Secret, swift, at times invisible, these nimble creatures oversee the daytime wanderers who journey into the unknown night. Actors who take these roles play smooth escape artists who slip into the underground, becoming shadows in plain sight and observing the awkward activities of the humans. Actors who enjoyed undercover work found these roles to be playful and challenging. Finally, the mechanicals, sensitive about any offense they may cause their audience, bumble through a script in which they alter the meaning entirely. These roles are wonderful for actors who want to develop comic timing. Combining these disparate elements into a coherent show was, at times, demanding.

We staged the show on a platform in the middle of the Civic Center's well-lit public area. We drew a considerable audience and were favorably reviewed. Unfortunately, the show lost much of the ambiance that had been achieved on the MCC stage through lighting and set design.

Kathy Keena and Clark Bowlen with the *Midsummer's Night Dream* set.

The duke (John Crowley) urges Hermia (Lucy Hurston) to recognize the maturity and guidance of her father Egeus (Michael McGunnigle). Meanwhile, Demetrius (Robert Mascarenas), her betrothed, listens. Lysander (Steve Smith), her true love, waits in the shadows. Lighting and set design by Clark Bowlen.

Puck (Debra Walsh) looks on as Oberon (John Crowley) and Titania (Gretchen Gubelman) argue. Fairies/rappers Tom Hogan and Lemon Slice listen in. Lighting and set design by Clark Bowlen.

The Mechanicals (left to right) Moonshine (Jason Vendrillo), Peter Quince (Jeffrey Paris), Thisbe (Andres Milliot), Pyramus (Ted Wohlsen), and Wall (Ian Martin) rehearse their play. Lighting and set design by Clark Bowlen.

(left to right) Fairy/rapper Besha Rodell looks on as Bottom (Ted Wohlsen) dons a Reagan mask provided by Titania (Gretchen Gobelman). Fairy/rapper (Elizabeth Reynolds) admires his new look. Lighting and set design by Clark Bowlen.

1994: *All Sunsets Look Alike* by Steve Starger

Background

I was not the only director who worked with Clark at the college. (I was the only director to work with him annually on a major production.) Other directors included Joan Baker, Bill Laurel, Mike McGunnigle and Julie Murtha. Occasionally, Clark himself directed a show.

Shakespeare Hartford produced a third show, *Romeo and Juliet*, directed by Lucy Hurston. I functioned as an advisor to the production. Once again, we performed in downtown Hartford, this time on Main Street, drawing a sizable lunchtime crowd. The actors were Bloomfield High School students and delivered a precocious performance.

Following *Midsummer*, due to my brother's death and the extreme demands of that production, I returned to graduate school, completing a second master's degree in spring 1993, this time in counseling arts. The following year I accepted the position of partial hospital coordinator at New Directions Outpatient Dual Diagnosis Facility. It was not until 1994, when Steve Starger's *All Sunsets Look Alike* was approved for production, that I returned to the theater department to direct.

The short script, only twenty pages long, spanned cultures and generations of unaddressed family dysfunction. Steve had been inspired by his actress cousin, whom he envisioned would play the part of Belle. For Clark and I, working with Steve was the beginning of a mutually creative connection that culminated in some of the best work of our artistic lives together. Shows included *The Man Who Became Trotsky, Cohen, Who By Fire*, and *Slick Sleeves*. Steve and I also produced a film in Clark's memory, *Ned and Alyce*.

Synopsis

All Sunsets Look Alike takes us to the Los Angeles home of a sixty-something Jewish widow, Belle, who has recently lost her mother, Sarah. Rather than abide by her mother's wishes—to be buried in Florida under spectacular sunsets—Belle has violated Judaic law by cremating her. Sarah had fled Russian Cossacks with other family members at age fourteen, after repeatedly being raped by the soldiers, who were killing the Jewish population. As the play opens, we do not yet know the full meaning of Sarah's beloved sunsets, which is shorthand for "avoiding the family shame of your damaged brother." Belle's brother, Sam, became mentally handicapped before puberty. He was institutionalized, although his placement was never discussed at home. The family made trips to Florida from the Bronx to escape the pain, eventually erasing him entirely from their lives. Only Belle remained in contact with Sam, who never understood why his parents abandoned him. Belle believes that her parents were so disappointed with Sam that the love they felt for each other died. Her resentment toward her mother is particularly deep.

Belle lives in Los Angeles on her own in a small home with few extras. Her only companion is her deceased husband. Their grown daughter has married an Arab and lives in Morocco. Belle is in her bathrobe, drifting off to sleep in the living room, when she hears someone break in through the kitchen door. Anita, a teenage girl with a knife, enters, planning to rob the house. Finding Belle awake and alert, Anita crumples instantly, admitting she doesn't know what to do next. She compulsively babbles on about her abusive boyfriend and her fear that he will seriously harm her. Anita has left home because her father has been committing incest with her since she turned twelve, and she had to run away. Belle listens, not without compassion, then asks Anita why she is throwing her life away on another abusive man who doesn't love her. Anita is confused by Belle's concern and takes the samovar that contains Sarah's ashes. She orders Belle to remain seated until she leaves, but not before confronting Belle about why there are no family pictures in the house. "Something's wrong here," she concludes before leaving. As Belle is upstairs calling the police, Anita returns the samovar with the message to Belle to "do something nice for your mother. She did the best she could."

Challenges

The set required no construction. A sofa and chair on stage suggests Belle's home. Her living-room wall is decorated with a painting of a sunset over the ocean. *Sunsets* does require, however, an understanding of cultural and generational differences and the ensuing potential for miscommunication. Combine that with the violation of privacy and property that is perpetrated on anyone whose home is broken into, and violence may be imminent. We used 10,000 Maniacs' "Trouble Me" for a musical counterpoint.

Actors

This is not a story about ordinary people. It is about two extraordinary survivors who face the difficult moral challenge of confronting each other and ultimately themselves. Rather than ending tragically, the unlikely encounter moves from violation and mistrust to a gradual softening of boundaries and an emphasis on the values both women share, creating a hopeful world for both. Belle's best days are over—she has lost her husband, mother, and daughter—and has seen her parents abandon her brother. She expresses her sorrow in ironic humor. Seeing another woman in an unworthy situation triggers her natural empathy and compassion. Belle's task is to thaw from emotional deep freeze and see another as worthwhile and deserving. To do so, she must set aside her own self-pity and reach out to Anita, her potential violator, thus opening her heart to forgive other mistreatment in her life.

Anita readily admits she is being used. Since this is not news to her, when Belle points this out, she is merely confused. Her father has repeatedly raped her, and her boyfriend uses her to commit crimes. Her life has been about survival. She does not know what to do when she is treated with kindness. The actress playing Anita has to be consistently surprised by Belle's concern and warmth. Anita slowly absorbs Belle's logic, which challenges her self-destructiveness. She is unaware of her right to an independent life, and believes her boyfriend protects her from worse horrors. Because she feels so unloved and defined by others, she is defensive. Belle shares this quality and identifies with Anita's emotional abandonment. Both characters balance on a tightrope between panic and trust.

Anita (Tracey Rakoczy) explains her not-too-
happy life to Belle (Lila Beldock Cohen).

1995: *Dutchman* by Amiri Baraka

Background

Following the success of *Sunsets*, Clark and I spoke to Steve about the
possibility he might follow up with a full-length script. An extremely
humble man, Steve insisted he was no playwright. As the arts and
culture critic for the local paper, his theater experience was far ranging.
Nevertheless, we tabled the idea for the time being. Clark asked me what
I wanted to direct. I suggested *Dutchman* by Amiri Baraka, provided
that I play the part of Lula. I wanted to direct the play for numerous
reasons. It was a concise piece of social literature, specifically addressing
racial inequity in America. The script was beautifully structured. The
symbolism was rich, yet it could be translated into specific characters
if carefully crafted. For the male role, I had in mind a colleague from
Naugatuck Community College, a full professor of English, actor, and

playwright, Bill Foster. I wanted to play Lula because she is as great a villainess as Lady Macbeth and a magnificent role. We were no longer twenty, but because our ages were close, I knew we could make it work.

This one-act play made LeRoi Jones, later Amiri Baraka, famous in 1964. The brief script had a playing time of probably forty minutes. I did not read it until high school, at least four years after it was written. I was immediately struck by its conciseness. In one act, something I knew to be true had been succinctly shown, without extraneous packaging to make it more palatable. Brevity is also the downside of the play; it tends to create an abstract lesson rather than a realistic event, which has to be counteracted on stage for the work's full power to be experienced.

Clark supported shows with cultural relevancy and readily agreed to the production. *Dutchman* was our second two-actor show to challenge cultural assumptions. However, here, the stakes were much higher, and there was no redeeming compassion.

Synopsis

A thirty-year-old white woman named Lula stands on a subway platform and spots a well-dressed, twenty-year-old black man, Clay, seated in the subway car. She smiles at him; he makes the mistake of smiling back. She boards the subway, finding her way to his seat. After taunting him about passing as a white man, which he misjudges as harmless, she urges him to bring her to the party to which he is headed. After the party, she explains, they will go back to her place and have sex. He eagerly agrees to her proposal. What she doesn't explain is the price, the total degradation of his character, which she methodically attacks with outrageous racial slurs, until his composure is lost. Confronted with his elemental self, he must tell her the truth; she knows nothing about blackness. Black hates her. Black wants to kill her. Not realizing he is in the realm of a pathological killer, he utters the words that will bring about his death. He has threatened her with violence. For this he will pay the ultimate price. Subway passengers, witnesses to the murder, collude in his death and even help her dump the body. As audience, it is our responsibility to recognize that this scenario is repeated endlessly without consequences for the murderess.

Clay, the symbol of black America—his name carries a biblical allusion to the Garden—is seduced by the appealing allure of white mainstream America, which claims to understand his plight but chastises him for pretending to be part of mainstream culture. White America, represented by Lula, is a pathological liar and murderer, waiting to bait the black man and trigger his outrage. This is his downfall. Once he reveals his raw anger, white America is justified in suppressing him, even destroying him. White America is, in fact, the snake in the Garden of Eden. Lula entices Clay with apples, which he eats. In the biblical fall from grace, the woman tempts the man with the forbidden fruit. Here, white America is the undefined evil of suppression, control, and sexual manipulation operating under the guise of presumed equality.

Challenges

Performance, however, does not translate from archetype. Casting is specific to people, and the more specific, the better. I was interested, therefore, in finding a particular type of man and woman to play the Dutchman and Lula roles. Individuality is paramount to counterbalance Lula's claims that Clay is a stereotypical black intellectual, and it would be a mistake to cast Lula as an identifiable toxic threat. Although it is tempting to create Lula as a villain, she must appear innocuous. It is her presentation of harmlessness that affords her the ability to position herself as a murderess. This "regular girl" convinces the subway passengers that it is sensible to help her dispose of the body. Lula is "one of us" while Clay becomes the stranger. The camouflage she accuses Clay of hiding behind is nothing compared to her disguise as a law-abiding citizen. While Clay admits he wears his suit to keep himself from attacking his oppressors, Lula wears bright, skimpy clothes to infiltrate enemy lines.

As mentioned above, my first choice for Clay was Bill Foster, a gifted actor. Although he was not age twenty, as the script required, if he accepted the role of Clay, I would play Lula, and we would create an older, adult version of *Dutchman*. While the show might seem to require little tech, light and sound are key. Clark located sound cues of shrieking hydraulic subway brakes and subway doors snapping open and shut. Combine those sounds with a hellish yellow hue of underground lighting that randomly shorts out and blinks back on, and you have the effect of a waking nightmare without escape.

Additional sound came from an infusion of music. Who better than the ultimate voice of soul, James Brown, synonymous with the 1960s empowerment of black people, relentless perseverance, and triumph through unfathomable difficulties and discrimination. The music would illustrate the impotence of black power against white America, the way the playwright uses the elderly black conductor who tips his hat to Lula, unaware she has murdered Clay just moments before. The show opens with "It May be the Last Time" combined with the shriek of brakes and the opening of the doors. Lula appears. The second music cue, "Man's World," coordinates with Lula's comment, "May people accept you as a ghost of the future. And love you, that you might not kill them when you can," and another subway stop. On Clay's line "Just strummin' and hummin' all day," the music cue "Think" is introduced. This portion of the script leads to the escalation that becomes deadly. Lula throws things into the aisle, hysterical, and asks Clay to dance the nasty with her. "Funky Good Time" is cued, and Lula bumps, grinds, and taunts Clay with lines like "Ten little niggers sitting on a limb, but none of them ever looked like him." Lula continues her wild dancing and shouting until Clay grabs her and tells her to sit down. Sound cue goes out. Clay finally tells her what she has stomped over. She can't wait. But she is also waiting to be seen as the person who peels away his disguise and reveals his authentic identity. She wants the same from him. When he is unable to recognize her as his white oppressor, she has no further use for him. He is disposable. And his own powerlessness will help her destroy him.

Actors

Rather than create a generic white woman, I developed Lula as a self-destructive individual. I added a history of severe sexual abuse, a hatred of white men, and the magical belief that only a black man could restore her self-worth by avenging the power of the white man. If a black man refuses to assist her, she considers herself betrayed and justified in killing him. Lula uses the American bias that black men are inappropriately sexual with white females to encourage passengers to help her dump his body. Clay fatally misconstrues her sexually taunting as harmless flirting.

In his character preparation, Bill created a tolerant, conventional male, initially attracted to Lula's lack of inhibition. He has had a lifetime of carefully cultivating himself as a sophisticated gentleman. He is fair-minded and expects fairness in return. Because he sees himself as an intellectual, Lula's escalating indiscretions seem merely foolish and self-destructive. Clay is elegant, well-dressed in an expensive suit, and impeccably groomed.

In contrast, Lula is carelessly and suggestively dressed or undressing. Playing Lula, I realized she wants Clay to kill her. If she gets him murderously mad, maybe she won't survive, and this will set her free. But as Clay explains, he won't kill anyone. The history of black rage is bound inside the blues, and Lula survives. Her final music is "Please, Please, Please" as her next victim comes into sight.

The show played at the Naugatuck Valley Community College where Bill Foster was teaching and Manchester Community College, where Clark and I taught. Student discussions followed both runs, to balance the brutality of the play and discuss its symbolic and literary value. Although written in 1964, it still has the power to shock.

Clay (Bill Foster) is enticed by the apple offered by Lula
(Kathleen Keena). Lighting and set design by Clark Bowlen.

Clay (Bill Foster) watches in amazement as Lula (Kathleen Keena) flips her head back at him in scorn. Lighting and set design by Clark Bowlen.

Clay (Bill Foster) tries to contain Lula's (Kathleen Keena) outrage as she berates him for trying to pass as a white man. Lighting and set design by Clark Bowlen.

1996: *The Man Who Knew Trotsky* by Steve Starger

Background

By 1996, Clark had made it his practice to allow me to choose our next artistic project. I hoped to direct O'Neill's *Long Day's Journey into Night* and proposed the show. Now a licensed mental health and addictions therapist, I recognized how accurately the script dramatized the downward spiral of family addiction. The disease progression is so predictable that the scrambling of scenes would highlight identifiable stages of destruction. My concept was scenes played inside oversized picture frames, with one framed scene performed and faded as another from an opposing angle was lit and unfrozen into action. Both Clark and I were excited about the prospect of deconstructing O'Neill, and Clark said he'd begin designing.

It might have been the following day that Steve and I spoke on the phone. I explained my family album concept and nonsequential scene work. Steve was enthused by the idea, but surprised me by saying, "You want a family play? I've got a family play for you!" I was amazed because I didn't know that he would ever consider writing a full-length script, especially for our upcoming production. The three of us discussed timetables, logistics, the family album set concept, and the excitement of Steve developing an original script. We agreed to meet regularly to monitor script progress. As director, I would work with Steve on character development so I could understand family members as specifically as he imagined them. We agreed to maintain the nonlinear structure I proposed. For Clark and I, this was a critical step in our collaboration. Adding a third person to our team energized and expanded our creativity. We were fortunate to have found a like-minded artist with whom we shared a mutual regard.

Synopsis

The bitter, dying father (Abe) of an immigrant Russian Jewish family holds a secret and cannot communicate with his loved ones. His younger son, Phil, a writer, longs to understand. He asks Abe to talk about his life, hoping to uncover the truth about the wound his father carries but can't reveal.

Steve used many devices to accommodate the nonlinear concept. In performance, this became a film-like production, with cuts from one vivid scene to another. At times, we used the framed scenes to create a montage of photos and cross talk in which a line from one actor became the cue for another actor's scene to begin.

Another wonderful aspect of the script is the Trotsky of Abe's imagination, present and witness to every scene. Trotsky functions as Abe's conscience, and, in the end, is the only one to convince him to do the responsible thing and explain what actually happened. According to family lore, Steve's father's reported seeing Trotsky riding the Bronx subway during his short stay in New York. It had become family myth, but had the quality of a tall tale. Steve began thinking about other family lore that may not have been authentic. What is valuable about heritage and worth taking into the future? What if one's family is full of jealousy, pettiness, and favoritism? Do we buy into the family angle or look to ourselves to create our identities? This was Steve's motivation for creating the script.

Abe provides details of his brother Morris's death with major variations; it was raining cats and dogs, or it was a clear night. Morris was shot in the heart, or the back of the head. He was shot by a gang, or by a lone gunman. Older son Danny remembers Abe's gambling debts and suspects he was seeing other women. He is certain of one thing, Dad tells a different story every time. He advises Phil to abandon his family history project and accept that their father will never be a reliable historian. *The Man Who Knew Trotsky* explores the lies we are told by our families, those we create about ourselves, and the collateral damage done in the process. It is about the justification of less than honorable behavior. The result is the family album, which must finally be decoded. The play also asks the audience to look at Abe, and by implication, our elders, as fallible people with fears, insecurities, and small-mindedness, which we all inherit as surely as we do the more noble aspects of our backgrounds.

Challenges

In retrospect, this show facilitated our break with more traditional theater. We brought in a playwright to accommodate a concept that was already in place. The non-chronological sequence was borrowed from cinema.

The conceit of still photos coming to life had the effect of "unfreezing" family memories through re-animation. It also suggested the broader concept of delving behind fixed memories to explore and question their larger reality. We developed and videotaped the background stories of the families beyond the scripted play, which expanded the work to a more experiential level for the actors.

For example, we filmed a mock-up of Philip and Rosemarie's wedding ceremony. In another segment, Philip and Daniel go bowling for the afternoon, to show the brothers before their subsequent conflict. We invited extra actors for the video segments to broaden the family experience beyond the immediate text of the play. The history of Abe and Lotte was a long story of thwarted ambition and dashed hopes, some of which were improvised to give the actors a sense of disappointment, disillusionment, and regret. Steve and I met at a Borders bookstore to discover and deepen the characters together. Each character had a personality profile, and we speculated what characters would do if confronted by various circumstances. We teased out, for example, a family history of Abe and Lotte's early courtship and marriage. All filmed improvisation became part of the family album, playing on video in the lobby pre-show and through intermission. We expanded our creativity by welcoming another artist and enhanced our production with a fresh perspective that synergized with our own.

Clark's set featured frames large enough to accommodate several people. The frames were off balance and damaged, to reflect memory's distortion of events. Lighting focused first on the scene taking place in the present, then shifted to another part of the stage to focus on a scene often occurring in parallel time. The show concludes with a family Seder; Philip offers a toast, observed by the absent Abe and his higher self, Trotsky. The show featured original music by Bill Walach of the Morgans, which included an arresting tuba performance. Bill had the distinction of having been commissioned to premiere new works for the mandolin by Klezmer musician Andy Statman, among others.

Actors

Phil, the youngest son, is the protagonist and narrator, and the action is seen from his perspective. He has been fed the same cover-up story as other family members, yet he wants to believe there is sacrifice beneath his father's tormented evasions. His motivation is to save his family. Yet Phil, as idealistic as he is, conducts an affair with his brother's girlfriend, betraying his wife and brother.

Older brother Danny does not hold Phil's illusions. Danny has little time or energy for family matters and remains detached, avoiding pain. His slick confidence hides an inner emptiness, which has a negative impact on his ability for emotional intimacy. Danny mirrors Abe in this aspect.

Lotte, Abe's wife, is a long-suffering, loyal partner whose innocence intensifies Abe's self-hatred.

In directing actors, it was of utmost importance to emphasize lifelong relationships of the family as a unit, the unmentionable secret, and consequential adjustments by family members. Their behaviors include unspoken agreements to avoid challenging Dad or upsetting Mother and to ignore the cloud of depression hanging over Abe. Rather, the goal has been to project a well-adjusted, loving family to the world. Of course, reality would break through intermittently, and someone, such as Lotte, would have an emotional meltdown trying to balance the contradictions. The album concept dramatically revealed flaws in the mythical family system. Extensive improvisation bonded cast members as a cohesive unit essential to the production.

Abe (David Gerstein) records his memories on tape for his son while his alter ego, Trotsky (Herman Shemonsky), listens downstage. Lighting and set design by Clark Bowlen.

Trotsky (Herman Shemonsky) is silent as Philip (Dan Tapper) struggles with his thoughts. Lighting and set design by Clark Bowlen.

(left to right) Lotte (Freddi Rabinowitz), Abe (David Gerstein), Rosemarie (Kathryn Page), Philip (Dan Tapper), Yvonne (Harriett Canty), and Dan (Christopher Jones) begin their Seder. Lighting and set design by Clark Bowlen.

1997: *Who By Fire*, edited by Mark Baker with Company Members

Background

> "Who By Fire"
>
> And who by fire, who by water, who in the sunshine,
> who in the nighttime?
> And who shall I say is calling?
>
> —Leonard Cohen, 1974

While we were working on *The Man Who Knew Trotsky*, I had been diagnosed and was being treated with chemotherapy for breast cancer. My diagnosis had a strong impact on Clark, who had never known me to have health issues. When I was forty-one, that changed, and it occurred to us for the first time that our life plans might not be under our control. I handled the situation by channeling my feelings into our art. I was reminded of my brother's death at age thirty-five and wanted to pay tribute to him while I still could. I proposed a project focused on veterans as our next endeavor. Clark agreed to start the project in the fall, but first proposed marriage when I completed my radiation treatment that summer. Our marriage was a formality since we had been living together for years. However, it symbolized our mutual commitment as we recognized we might lose each other.

I wanted a show that honored not only deceased veterans but also those who had survived combat but were struggling emotionally with unseen battle scars. John began his military career during the de-escalation of United States involvement in Vietnam. He had achieved the rank of captain with army airborne and was a member of Special Forces at the time of his death in 1991.

Clark and I called the project a "living newspaper" and advertised for Vietnam veterans who wanted to tell their stories. Our original concept was to have multiple televisions on stage broadcasting news footage about Vietnam, with commentary by newscasters and politicians. I searched for first-person accounts of combat and found Mark Baker's *Nam*, which provided a range of diverse voices veterans could portray. We received permission from Baker's publisher to use monologues from the collection, and we soon had a rough outline.

The veterans featured in *Who By Fire* were former marine point man Harold "Butch" Donle and combat medic Dave Ionno. Both were active members of the Veterans Education Project, an outreach group that spoke to high-school students about the realities of combat service. Joining them was veteran Eddy Kaytis, a versatile actor who took on a wide range of characters. Dan Tapper was assistant director and also stepped in to play auxiliary characters as needed. Finally, Steve Starger wrote and performed a monologue that recalled his teaching English to Puerto Rican servicemen for combat preparation.

Synopsis

To open, the cast began with their backs to the audience, staring at their reflections mirrored in a replica of the Vietnam Memorial Wall as Leonard Cohen's "Who By Fire" plays. Because Vietnam veterans were mature men by 1997, their presence on stage was arresting. On cue, they turn in military formation, and march forward, as if stepping away from the confines of the Wall and toward the audience. This established our intention to represent the spirits of living and dead warriors.

The show begins with the veterans asking collectively, "Do you want to hear a genuine war story?" from the introduction of Mark Baker's *Nam*, and its response is "I only know Vietnam as a story. It's not like I was there." The material includes monologues, scenes, and a narrative that introduces American boyhood as a time of pretending to be war heroes by killing bad guys, graduating to physical competition between peers, and then acquiring the stoicism required to become a man. With each description, actors dramatize the stages. Postwar scenes all contain themes of coming back home changed, finding it impossible to convey their experiences to family and friends, and feeling isolated. Stories included a POW and several wounded warriors—some trying to adjust to civilian life, others struggling to manage employment.

Butch contributed several original pieces of writing, including one about an ambush he survived and another about a young Vietnamese barber who had volunteered his services to Butch's platoon. It was only after the barber's death that Butch learned he was Viet Cong. Another piece of material came from the Department of Veterans Affairs' (VA) description of PTSD and a first-person narrative describing symptoms such as sleeplessness, nightmares, flashbacks, sudden anger, loss of concentration, relationship difficulties. It was easy to adapt this into a discussion between fellow veterans at a vet center.

Challenges

Clark designed a set that emotionally expressed the content of the show. He stretched reflective material across three panels to represent the Wall, and when the structure was lit, the actors facing the panels were in sightline of the audience. Clark built the set with the idea that we would travel it, and we—the veterans, Clark, and me—mounted the installation and broke it down at each site to provide symbolism. The other symbol was a fire pit at center stage, which filled the stage with smoke during the firefight. We later used this fire as the unifying anchor for the homeless vet scene. The television monitors did not make it into production. Although the concept was exciting, performances quickly became the focus of rehearsal, and we decided the screens would detract from the live action on stage. Locations included town halls, vet centers, backyards, and bars—places veterans were likely to gather. A different musical selection, always from the era, often blues or rock, and relevant to the material that followed, opened each scene. Butch, who had his own radio show with Dave Ionno at Central Connecticut State University, was responsible for the score. All of the music was appropriate to Vietnam in either period or theme.

We were fortunate to be able to tour the show to veterans' homes in New Britain, Rocky Hill, and West Haven after major struggles with bureaucratic red tape. We were surprised by the many channels of approval we had to pass through. In retrospect, I believe the VA did not want to disturb PTSD patients by triggering unmanageable memories. Although we had dealt with this thoroughly with the performers during the rehearsal process, we were not as attuned to the veteran audience. It turned out that veterans' home residents were grateful we had provided a creative, healing experience by reframing their combat service with reverence. The impact on performers was positive, and for some, opened a window previously shut on that part of their lives. For the civilian audience, the show was educational, providing some idea of the mental and emotional price of wartime service, although we were unable to convey this fully on stage.

Vietnam veterans were shamed and isolated once they returned home. They were not welcomed but were blamed for the war, despite the fact that many young warriors had been taught that service was the only honorable decision. Because of the huge objections to a mandatory draft, antiwar resistance overwhelmed the country. Military personnel were stereotyped as heartless killers despite the enormous risks, loss of life, and lifelong emotional trauma that resulted from the horrific circumstances. It is a national tragedy that we do not honor the warriors we sent to fight and die so the rest of us may be spared. No one hates war more than its warriors. For a second time, we created an original show, this time with a nonactor population, to introduce a social issue others were not addressing.

Actors

The veterans who performed in the show were not actors, except for Eddy Kaytis. In multiple ways, this worked to our advantage. Their honesty and lack of affectation enhanced believability. After all, these were the people who had been there. Who better to tell the story? It is imperative that anyone who works with veterans understands that such work is painful and demanding and requires a good deal of preparatory healing to remain emotionally grounded. I have seen veterans regain lost memories recounting situations that have eluded them until they dramatize the details. The work is rewarding but must be practiced delicately and with reverence for process, which needs to be more highly valued than product. This may be frustrating when you are trying to put together a show, but that's the first rule of veterans theater. The rehearsal must be stopped if a cast member is having emotional difficulty. If a person is staring off blankly into space, chances are he or she is in the middle of a flashback; bring the person back by reorienting him or her to current circumstances—such as a location, activity, safety level, companions, and time—and giving permission to discontinue the practice. It is unadvisable to continue when anyone's safety issues are at risk, and, as any artist knows, you will never get creative work from people trying to protect themselves. This is true with any psychic material, but trauma work results makes people more vulnerable, and establishing and sustaining trust are the most important elements in veterans theater.

Some people involved with this work were the VA counselors in West Haven, Connecticut, site of PTSD combat treatment, where Clark and I visited a treatment graduation. We observed two critical elements of healing. The first was witnessing without judgment. This is the telling of stories, without justifying actions, which leaves room to grieve tragedy, deal with unforeseen outcomes and address survivor guilt and other burdens veterans carry silently. The second is the power of symbolism to express the universality of the war experience through common images, circles of fellowship, and military ceremonies used to honor war dead. For Clark and me, it was a privilege to share in the emotional lives of veterans, who carry our national grief. This show strengthened our commitment to social issues in theater.

(left to right) Dave Ionno, Butch Donle, and Eddy Kaytis face the Wall with their backs to the audience as their images reflect outward. They will turn in military formation and march forward as if stepping from their reflections. Lighting and set design by Clark Bowlen.

(left to right) Eddy Kaytis looks on as Butch Donle recounts an ambush in which his American Indian friend Doc (Dave Ionno) was killed. Lighting and set design by Clark Bowlen.

(left to right) Dave Ionno, Butch Donle, and Eddy Kaytis are served by a bartender (Dan Tapper) as they recall their warrior days. Lighting and set design by Clark Bowlen.

(left to right) Eddy Kaytis, Butch Donle (covered by camouflage blanket), and Dave Ionno gather around an outdoor fire pit in the scene "Homeless Vets." Lighting and set design by Clark Bowlen.

CHAPTER 3
FINAL COLLEGE YEARS, 1998 TO 2001

This chapter focuses on our final years at the college. Of those years, 1998 was the most innovative and expansive of our legacy. By that point, we had moved to progressively original scripts, beginning with Steve Starger's *All Sunsets Look Alike* and *The Man Who Knew Trotsky*. The *Who By Fire* Vietnam veterans show was also a departure from traditionally scripted theater. We had adapted published veteran interviews, stringing them into a coherent production with thematic linking, narration, and symbolic unity. By this time, Clark and I were enthused about unique approaches to often overlooked topics.

Each summer, Clark and I would pack up the Honda and drive to Ontario for the Stratford Shakespeare Festival, inspired by viewing the work of the directors and artists we most admired. During the twelve- to thirteen-hour drive, we listened to Laurie Anderson, Kronos, Leonard Cohen, Tom Waits, or—if I were driving and Clark was agreeable—Clapton. On one such drive, Clark praised Cohen's writing talent. He was impressed by Cohen's Judaic melodies, sublime instrumentation, and carefully crafted lyrics, which celebrate beauty and are equally appropriate as poetry. His articulation and phrasing are precise, and he intends his recordings to be thoughtfully consumed. For many vocalists, sound is primary, and meaning secondary. Cohen sings to tell his story, and music facilitates him. This makes him eminently theatrical, since all theater is storytelling. He also acknowledges the horrors of which mankind is capable. Songs like "Everybody Knows," "Story of Isaac," "The Future," and "Anthem" explore the darker aspects of humanity some prefer to avoid. His astonishment over the beauty of life and dual existentialism informed our work, much like Shakespeare, Williams, Miller, Brecht, Laurie Anderson, and Robert Wilson. We discussed the possibility of a Cohen-inspired production, but only as a concept. In Ontario, where Cohen's literature and music is available in almost every bookstore, we purchased what we did not own. The development of our Cohen musical resulted in some of our most innovative work.

James McLure's *Lone Star/Laundry and Bourbon* provided a complete departure from the tremendous scale and coordination of a musical. The play is a small but heart-wrenching production about a couple estranged by the husband's combat experience. As husband Roy struggles with alcoholism and despair, his wife Elizabeth's frustration grows. Roy hopes to return to his prewar past, but is challenged by his love for Elizabeth to face life in the present.

Our final performance at the college was Oliver Goldsmith's *She Stoops to Conquer*, a seventeenth-century classic to which we applied our Stratford education. Drawing room comedy is a specialty of the Shakespeare Festival, and having seen the best actors and directors' work with similar material, we frolicked, as much as possible, knowing it was our final college production. I have added one community theater show, *Crimes of the Heart*, to this section. We were invited in 2001 to direct and design the show for the Mark Twain Masquers. This work eased our transition from college to community theater.

1998: *Came So Far for Beauty: The Music of Leonard Cohen*

Background

I had never directed a musical. Clark, on the other hand, was familiar with musical productions. He explained that we would bring in a musical director and cast actors who could also sing. *Cohen* was the first of three musicals we produced, but it was the most personal for us. My only musical experience had been as an audience member, watching outdated 1950s scores with performers indicating, overacting, and breaking into song at the most unlikely times. I couldn't imagine serious work being accomplished in this genre. But Clark was sure there was another way to approach it. I agreed to research Cohen and at least think about how to find a way into the material.

After reading Cohen's *Beautiful Losers*, *The Favorite Game*, *Selected Poems 1956–1968*, *Book of Mercy*, *Stranger Music*, *Intricate Preparations*, and the biographies *Various Positions* and *A Life in Art*, and listening to his musical releases, which were also published as poems, I was able to conceptualize the structure of a production. We invited Steve Starger, our theater collaborator and also an excellent musician, to be our arranger. Deborah Simmons, the college's music chair, became music director. Herman Shemonsky, who had played Trotsky in Steve's play and had a magnificent singing voice, became the mature Cohen.

Synopsis

Considering the range of musical styles employed by Cohen, I saw his work in phases of development. My idea was that his mature self would observe and comment on the attitudes and actions of his younger self. At times, his mature self would intervene in an attempt to warn or convince his younger self about looming mistakes, often resulting in a power struggle between the two. Younger Cohen would sing his early songs, and mature Cohen would step in with later lyrics, challenging his naïve view. The resulting duets worked well.

The first phase was the folk music/romantic voice of Cohen's young self, the writer of "Suzanne." We personified Suzanne as his muse, and she led him through the other life stages. She also functioned as stage manager, conducting scene changes, through the abandoned friend described in "Famous Blue Raincoat," the one-time lover of Chelsea Hotel resident Janis Joplin, and the rowdy cowboy self of "Closing Time." Suzanne narrated the literary passages from Cohen's prose, which was the only spoken material. The rest of the action was sung. The overarching concept was that the mature Cohen and his troupe are touring the concert *Came So Far for Beauty*. The troupe enters the empty stage and plays roles in the flashback scenes featuring his younger self.

In the opening sequence of act 2, younger Leonard is at the height of absurdity as he opens with "First We Take Manhattan," bathed in disco-ball lighting, his shirt collar suggestively open. The next number, "I'm Your Man," opens with Cohen seducing each of the backup singers. Halfway through, however, he recognizes that he is playing a part he cannot possibly live up to. The lyrics of "I'm Your Man" include the disclaimer, "I've been making you all these promises that a man just cannot keep." The younger Cohen has finally caught himself in his own bravado and now confronts his genuine self. Younger Cohen walks off the stage in disgust; meeting his mature self back stage. The backup singers are left confused until Suzanne rushes on, directing the company to get into costume for "Jazz Police" and perform it as a dance number.

As younger and mature Leonard face off, mature Leonard takes command, delivering "Everybody Knows" to his youthful persona. Young Leonard takes off his nightclub singer costume and changes into his tasteful dress of the mature artist. Here, pretense is dropped. This is the moment when Cohen—and by implication, all of us—stop fooling ourselves and face our dark, less lovable aspects, humbled by our insignificance. The crew strikes the mirrored set, the barroom tables and chairs, and the bed used in the first act for the Chelsea Hotel scene, and mature Leonard is left on a bare stage singing "Waiting for the Miracle" as the company's voices join him. The next number is "Came So Far for Beauty," which the younger and mature selves sing to each other as a duet. Young Leonard then joins the chorus. Mature Leonard sings "Tower of Song," perhaps from a stray ladder left during the set strike. Suzanne invites him to join her dance as the instrumental for "Dance Me to the End of Love" begins. He then gestures for her to be seated, as he delivers "Hallelujah." Suzanne summons the company to join in the chorus of Hallelujah," completing the show.

Challenges

Maintaining a plot with music and a few literary quotes was a directing challenge. Fortunately, I'd put the sequences together, so I had the advantage of knowing exactly what action was required to explain sequences without dialogue. This was accomplished by unobtrusively placing various props for different scenes against the back wall of the stage; they were taken to center stage only for the specific scene to be performed. Suzanne would direct the crew to move set pieces downstage and then strike them, preparing for the next sequence. The mature Leonard character would observe the action outside the performance space but on stage, a presence apart from the action. The wall would be broken only if he walked directly into a scene.

The flexibility of the set was the strongest feature of Clark's design. Upstage center, reflective panels disguised a dressing room that became visible with special lighting. On the bare stage, which the company "moves into" to occupy a set, scenes unfold representing different phases of Cohen's career. The set shifts to an empty stage again, as the company packs up amps and loads the truck for another stop on the tour. Arranging time for acting and musical rehearsals, designing, and practicing choreography were new complications. Live musicians added another scheduling requirement.

We were proud that people from England traveled to our theater to see the show, and our company was invited to Canada to perform an encore. Cohen himself sent us a special award for our success.

Actors

Method training and directing experience had taught me to cast actors capable of the broadest emotional range for character creation. Casting considerations for a musical, however, require skilled actors who can sing. A two-year community college does not have a large selection of students specializing in drama and music. Musicals don't necessarily call for world-class singers, but this show would be entirely sung and needed actors to carry multiple roles. We were bound to professional standards. Poor or weak singers would be as damaging as bad actors. I became aware of how many good actors had to be ruled out because they couldn't sing. Musicals were twice as labor intensive as drama. Drama and music rehearsals share available time. Only after a musical number had been practiced could I impose motivation and action into the scene. Since it isn't actually possible to work twice as fast, there was less time to work one on one with each actor. I worked most extensively with both Leonard characters, fine actors who provided emotional continuity to the overall production.

Suzanne (Melinda Kalmar) joins Young Leonard (Paul Pricer) in a duet of "Suzanne" as Mature Leonard (Herman Shemonsky) watches from the shadows. Lighting and set design by Clark Bowlen.

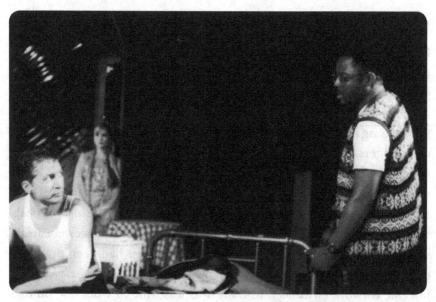

Young Leonard (Paul Pricer) says farewell to his male lover (James A Riley Jr.) in the number "Hey, That's No Way to Say Goodbye" as Suzanne (Melinda Kalmar) observes. Lighting and set design by Clark Bowlen.

Eddy Kaytis, Paul Pricer, and James A. Riley Jr. sing a spirited version of "Don't Go Home With Your Hard-On" as Herman Shemonsky (Mature Leonard) expresses his outrage. Jeri-Ann Burke-Nielson discreetly glances away. Lighting and set design by Clark Bowlen.

Young Leonard (Paul Pricer) is confronted by Mature Leonard (Herman Shemonsky) to "Come Back to the War" that is life. Lighting and set design by Clark Bowlen.

Backup singer Lori Beaulieu is charmed by Young Leonard (Paul Pricer) as he seductively serenades her. Lighting and set design by Clark Bowlen.

Mature Leonard (Herman Shemonsky) and
Suzanne (Melinda Kalmar) sing a duet.

Mature Leonard (Herman Shemonsky) gazes into the mirror and
sees the reflection of his muse, Suzanne (Melinda Kalmar).

The cast of *Came So far For Beauty* sings "Hallelujah": (left to right) Jeri-Ann Burke-Nielson, Eddy Kaytis, Andi Jackson, Herman Shemonsky, Lori Beaulieu, James A. Riley Jr. Lighting and set design by Clark Bowlen.

2000: *Lone Star/Laundry and Bourbon* by James McLure

Background

Clark and I did not collaborate on a production in 1999. Although we considered touring *Came So Far for Beauty*—we had been invited to the Montreal Arts Festival that year—logistics ruled it out. We were not a theater company, but a theater department of a community college, and student turnover was high. Many were part-time students, skipping semesters due to life circumstances. Our students generally had jobs and family and financial constraints. Those who remained had new academic studies. Despite the remarkable artistic success of the Cohen production, participation in the theater department was declining as was overall college enrollment. When class enrollment minimums were unmet, they were cancelled. The play production course, which provided technical support for department productions, used to fill without difficulty. Now, it had only four or five students, and it had become unprofitable. Although other departments also suffered low numbers, the arts programs were often most expendable. Composition and psychology courses, required courses for first semester students, remained full. However, those who hoped college was for them frequently dropped out after their initial semester.

In addition, despite the Humanities Department's public acknowledgment and congratulations on our marriage several years earlier, Clark was summoned by registered mail—while on a wilderness trip in Nova Scotia—to address a conflict of interest for our continuing work. This was a tremendous blow to him as was his consequent suspension from the college until the teachers' union interceded.

All these factors influenced our choice for our 2000 production: James McLure's *Lone Star/Laundry and Bourbon* was well written yet technically simple. McLure is a combat veteran who writes about postwar adjustment. *Who By Fire* had educated us about some of the ongoing difficulties of returning Vietnam veterans, and perhaps because we faced our own adjustments, we were drawn to those scripts.

Synopsis

In his production notes, McLure states, "It is my intention the two plays be performed together to make a full evening of theatre." Roy and Elizabeth are married but things haven't been the same since Roy returned from Vietnam two years before. In *Lone Star,* we join husband Roy for a typical evening at Angel's Bar in Maynard, Texas. *Laundry and Bourbon,* on the other hand, takes us to the back porch of their home in Maynard, where wife Elizabeth is busy folding laundry and passing the time with her neighbor, Hattie.

The women's play is presented first. Maynard is a small town and stifling hot. The air conditioning has failed at Elizabeth's, and Hattie has dropped in for respite from her three children. "Let's Make a Deal" is on TV, which Hattie spoils by revealing outcomes to Elizabeth. Hattie also has a lot to say about Roy's behavior and activities, including his ownership of a pink Thunderbird, the longing way young women look at him, and his wild attitude. The friends drink bourbon together, and Elizabeth sorrowfully confides Roy has been missing for two days. Roy can't hold onto a job and made her quit hers at the pharmacy. On top of that, she is pregnant. Another high-school acquaintance, Amy Lee, comes over to deliver an air conditioner part and announces that she saw Roy with another woman. Elizabeth quickly counters that he's told her all about it.

Although it is unclear what their future holds, it is clear Elizabeth will remain loyal to her lone star and will do everything she can to help him deal with the personal torment of Vietnam. McLure explains, "Elizabeth is intended to be the spiritual complement of Roy." By introducing the game show "Let's Make a Deal," the playwright may be asking if the deal--the consequences of war on their marriage and future–was fair for either of them.

Lone Star takes place behind Angie's Bar, a junkyard "where old worn-out things end up." Roy sits in the front seat of an abandoned car. He left high school a popular, athletic man, with a promising, quick mind and fondness for risk taking, to serve his country. Back now for two years, he is drunk every night. His brother Ray, younger, slower, and lovingly accepting, talks to him without trying to repair or change him. Ray claims the army rejected him for "football knee," but Roy says it was "football brain." Roy has returned a bitter and sullen alcoholic who longs for his prewar days. The magical affair that led to his marriage is betrayed as he philanders with other women, spends every night at the bar, and is unable to keep a job. He tells his brother their mother is senile and their father is a "damn fool." He confides that he has seen people without heads, a guy "stick an M-16 up a gook's cunt and fire it," and guys "burn babies." These war atrocities haunt him and are the reason he searches for his old friends. He yearns to unburden himself and receive absolution for his horrific experience.

Into this equation comes an unlikely variable. An envious classmate, Cletis (Amy Lee's husband), has taken Roy's beloved car on a joyride and destroyed the 1959 pink Thunderbird, Roy's symbolic connection to his past. Ray decides to break the news to him by first revealing a decidedly worse piece of news: he and Elizabeth slept together while Roy was in Vietnam. Ray explains how lonely they were without him. After an appropriate implosion, in which Ray gives his brother the opportunity to kill him, Roy is told about his destroyed car. Over the course of the evening, we learn how much Roy has missed the relationship he and Elizabeth shared, how difficult it has been to deal with life since he returned to Maynard, and that nothing has been the same for him since his return. What makes both plays blend so beautifully is that we are given enough information about Elizabeth and Roy to 1) care what happens to them, 2) want them to reconcile, 3) predict that Roy's admission of how much he loves Elizabeth will enable him to be more honest with her about his needs, and 4) recognize that Elizabeth will tell Roy about her pregnancy when he returns, which may move them into a more optimistic future.

I chose to direct the show to this conclusion: that the relationship is intact enough to be repaired, that Elizabeth is willing and able to be there for him, that Roy will be able to heal and reclaim his manhood. If Roy becomes a loving husband and father, they will persevere. Although the characters are not seen together on stage, they are very much a focus of each other's motivation. Both carry clear memories of past stability to inspire their visions of the future.

The play returned us to the trauma of combat survival and the multitude of displaced veterans who never adjusted and suffer from addiction, eruptions of anger, violence, mistrust of authority, and suicidal ideation. Unconditional acceptance from others and self-forgiveness are prerequisites to healing.

Challenges

Clark, as usual, designed a striking set to accommodate the production. For *Laundry*, Elizabeth's back porch was stage right of the thrust stage. A line of clothes hung between a rocking chair, a folding table, and several loose chairs. The actresses worked to convey physical fatigue due to the heat; Elizabeth's shirt was tied above her waist and her sleeves were rolled back. Her hair was hurriedly thrown up in a tie to keep it off her neck. All of the actresses were impatient and irritable, drinking, gossiping, and complaining. Clark's background was dark, so that the porch area was brightly lit, but the rest of the space melted into shadows. The effect was to create daylight in the corner they worked, beyond which was vast expanse.

Lone Star, stage left, was located behind the backdoor of Angel's bar, leading to an unkempt yard of abandoned articles. It is here that Roy feels the most at home. *Lone Star* takes place at night, and the lighting reflected the vividness of the Texas sky in a brilliant blue. Roy is the lone star of the evening, and it is also the name of the beer he drinks. As the backdoor of Angel's bar opened, a fragment of a country song would blare from inside and abruptly cease as the door slammed. With sound there would be bright yellowish light common to saloons. The two sides of the set uniformly matched, paralleling each other in angle, dimension, and significance.

Actors

The two casts—connected by intimacy, tragedy, and estrangement issues—rehearsed separately, aware of each other's process and progress. As foreign as it might seem to have no interaction between husband and wife, ex-lovers, men and women, the separation of casts offered some benefit to actors. For the women, it created an atmosphere of intimacy in which disappointment, vulnerability, and frustration could be freely expressed. They shared latent resentments and jealousies that would never be discussed in mixed company. We learn about Roy's failing marriage from the perspective of his wife, who reveals her abiding love for her seemingly hopeless husband.

Lone Star replays the same issues from a male perspective, in which the unbearable pain of the husband's combat memories overwhelms his ability to exist in the present. His agony is palpable as he continues drinking and becomes increasingly mentally and emotionally compromised. Roy's vulnerability is revealed through his progressive intoxication, in which he increasingly loses self-control, disclosing desperate fear. The roles for both main characters required an emotional catharsis accessible to astute actors.

Elizabeth (Mary Roberge), Amy Lee (Erin Fitzmaurice),
and Hattie (Carmen Canal) try to cool down on Elizabeth's
porch. Lighting and set design by Clark Bowlen.

Elizabeth (Mary Roberge) is put off by Hattie's (Carmen Canal) and Amy Lee's
(Erin Fitzmaurice) town gossip. Lighting and set design by Clark Bowlen.

Elizabeth (Mary Roberge, center) tries to break up Amy Lee (Erin Fitzmaurice) and Hattie (Carmen Canal) as they go after each other. Amy Lee has accused Hattie of having a baby outside of marriage. Lighting and set design by Clark Bowlen.

Ray (Brian Donlan) and Roy (Jared Ober) recall town life before Roy's service in Vietnam. Lighting and set design by Clark Bowlen.

Ray (Brian Donlan) and Roy (Jared Ober) plot to dramatize an example of Vietnam warfare. Lighting and set design by Clark Bowlen.

Roy (Jared Ober) sits on the seat of an abandoned car behind Angel's
Saloon, drinking Lone Star. Lighting and set by Clark Bowlen.

2001: *She Stoops to Conquer* by Oliver Goldsmith

Background

We would never know whether the college's sudden concern about a
conflict of interest related to our relationship was an attempt to push
Clark, a tenured professor, into early retirement. Prior to the notification
and the ensuing directive that we were no longer permitted to work
together, Clark had contracted my directing services for *She Stoops to
Conquer.* Since the contract had been approved prior to the notice, we
were allowed to proceed. Nevertheless, the show would be our final
one, after which the theater department would close. Clark would still
be a part of the Communications Division and teach acting courses, but
was now required to teach public speaking to retain his full-time status.
Clark was determined to make the best of his new situation, expressing
relief that he wouldn't have to work as hard as he had before. However,
the truth was that we were heartbroken. We had founded and developed
the program, progressing to increasingly sophisticated productions. Its
termination only inspired in us to make a greater commitment to our
immediate work.

She Stoops to Conquer, first performed in 1773, is a wonderful example of the English "comedy of manners". At Stratford, we had seen many such drawing room comedies, poking fun at the conventions of the day—including upper-class pretentiousness and the merit of appearance over content—and hypocrisies that audiences could identify in themselves (or at least their neighbors). It also employs many Elizabethan devices, such as tangled identities, misinformation, and role reversals. Young people teach their elders, who are exposed as self-serving. Love matches among young couples triumph over parental objections. Humor is derived from verbal dexterity, frequent puns, double meanings, innuendos, and nimble wit. Those who are most clever are the stars of stage. It is easy to miss meanings within the rapid-fire dialogue, which must be meticulously interpreted. We would need interpretive dexterity, timing, and comic sensibility.

Synopsis

Goldsmith's strength is his uncanny ability to see people's blind spots and illuminate how they thwart desires. Mr. and Mrs. Hardcastle, both in their second marriages, are parents of two adolescents. Mr. Hardcastle, a retired war hero, has a refined, eloquent daughter, Kate, who is uncommonly clever. Mrs. Hardcastle's son Tony is a spoiled, idle youth who drinks and enjoys practical jokes. What brought the two parents together is a matter best left undiscovered, but it seems to be working out. By mutual agreement, Mr. Hardcastle's friend, Mr. Marlow, is sending his son to the house to meet Kate, and potentially arrange a marriage between the two offspring, if the chemistry is right. We discover, through Kate's cousin, however, that young Marlow is terrifically shy with women of good breeding but forward with those of the lower class. Shattering illusions of grandeur and superiority held by the upper classes is a recurrent theme. Young Marlowe, used to being accommodated as a privileged son of a wealthy man, is at ease giving orders and commands to whomever he believes are his underlings. Troublemaking Tony misleads Marlow and his friend Hastings to believe they are visiting an inn rather than a private residence. Consequentially, Marlow treats his host as if he were a servant, much to the older man's disapproval. Marlow's inappropriateness includes interrupting his war stories, ordering him to bring punch, directing him to fetch the dinner menu, and making rude remarks about the food. Marlow expects his boots to be removed by Hardcastle and the older man to relinquish his seat by the fire. Meanwhile, Hastings—who has been advised by Kate's cousin, Miss Neville, whom he is courting, that they have been incorrectly told the house is an inn—flatters Mrs. Hardcastle by pretending to believe her son is her brother and that she must have been to London to acquire her taste in fashion. She is enchanted with the flattery.

Some of the play's most beguiling moments include Mrs. Hardcastle being led around the outside of the house in a carriage by Tony until she believes she is forty miles from home. Upon seeing a shadow, she falls to her knees, begging the presumed highwayman to spare her child. Baffled, her husband answers with more than a little annoyance, "What! Dorothy, don't you know me?" Another such moment occurs when Miss Neville, noticing Kate's distress, inquires, "Sure no accident has happened among the canary birds or goldfishes? Has your brother or the cat been meddling? Or has the last novel been too moving?" The implication is that manufactured dramas result from excessive pampering.

Challenges

We shifted Goldsmith's seventh-century comedy to the 1920s. This choice was whimsical, but *She Stoops to Conquer* also has a twentieth-century sensibility. Our costume concepts included fanciful touches, such as feather dusters for shoulder pads, silverware for lapels, and vines on the arms of the hostess to match her floral arrangements. Flapper costumes translated well; the 1920s were a time of overindulgence and privilege, which are satirized in the play. Clark's set included a main stage parlor room, where the guests were greeted and much of the central action takes place. Oversized, artless floral arrangements designed by Mrs. Hardcastle dominate the room. Other settings were the Three Pigeon's Pub, where son Tony spends his time and his mother's money; downstage left, this setting was represented with nondescript tables. The garden, a rendezvous location used by young men planning to win the hearts of young women, was appropriately romantic. Woven latticework draped in vines above a bench, center stage, replaced the parlor setting of earlier scenes. The musical selections were overly dramatic, with "Moonlight Sonata" playing during the scene in which Mrs. Hardcastle mistakenly believes she has been accosted by thieves. The carriage trip was played at the skirt of the stage with specials tracking precipitous movement. Fortunately, for everyone involved, our final production was high-spirited and upbeat.

Actors

Former Equity and SAG member Tony Valenches took the role of Mr. Hardcastle, bringing a wonderful humility and dignity to the character. Experienced actress Robin C'Miel played the easily excitable Mrs. Hardcastle. West African student Bernard Andoh was the entitled son. In stylized comedy, the language is critical. All actors are required to speak precisely and in a bold volume. Although there is certainly room for individual interpretation, most of the roles are stock characters. The

The cast of *She Stoops to Conquer* (left to right): Servant (Lance Earnest), Tony (Rick Biercheck), Miss Neville (Sarah Triano), Sir Charles (Mike McGunnigle), Mrs. Hardcastle (Robin C'Miel), Mr. Hardcastle (Tony Valenches), Maid (Joey Rosenthal), Miss Hardcastle (Kate Olis), Marlow (Bernard Andoh), and Hastings (Jared Ober). Lighting and set design by Clark Bowlen.

THE PLAY'S THE THING

drunkard remains drunk, and the foolish mother remains foolish. No cathartic experience shifts the characters toward greater awareness. Humor is derived from wit, and comic timing is essential. The pace must remain rapid, as if on fast-forward. Cast teamwork is crucial because every action depends on the one prior, and the actors cue each other within seconds. It is not the sort of script where actors can drop lines and pick up content later. I personally enjoy such stylized comedy because it demands so much from all the team members and requires tight cohesion as a group to play with maximum skill.

2001: *Crimes of the Heart* by Beth Henley

Background

Now disengaged from the college, I was fortunate to have some confidence expressing my philosophy, style and goals in directing. My college credentials carried some status. Clark's reputation as a respected community theater designer carried more. Several months after the 2001 spring semester, we heard that the Mark Twain Masquers board was in search of a director for its fall show, *Crimes of the Heart* by Beth Henley. Having just closed the MCC program, we were eager to invest our energy elsewhere. The project was an opportunity to dive into creative work. Clark was a fan of Henley's and assured me of her playwriting expertise. I would have been happy to direct the worst playwright in the world at that point. Fortunately, Henley's writing is wonderful.

The play had been written in 1981, when Henley was twenty-nine and unknown. *Crimes* earned her a Pulitzer Prize and Drama Critics Circle Award. By 2001, she was a nationally renowned playwright, whose plays included *The Miss Firecracker Contest, The Wake of Jamey Foster, The Debutante Ball, Abundance, The Lucky Spot, Impossible Marriage,* and *Control Freaks*. Henley, born in Jackson, Mississippi, compares her early plays, including *Crimes*, to what Tennessee Williams termed "memory plays" (like the *Glass Menagerie*). She writes about the "amber glow" of these plays, which I interpret as a nostalgic longing for the closeness shared in the midst of unrepeatable and, in some sense, preposterous

85

circumstances. It may be that the heightened reality brings characters in closer proximity to their authentic selves and therefore allows us to see their moral convictions, or lack there of.

Henley has an unerring pitch for the false courtesy and gracious overstatement of Southern gentility, especially when expressed by women to manipulate others. Calling others "sweet potato" and "angel food " reduce a person to a dish to be consumed, rendering one simultaneously charmed and resentful. This strategy, which still makes men helpless victims, perpetuates the double standard of woman as fragile "belles." If there is any doubt why women are treated like dim-witted children, look no further than *Crimes of the Heart*. Henley's tongue-in-cheek playfulness translates into some good comedy. Mark Twain, with his love of satire to expose pretensions, would have approved of the play.

Synopsis

Crimes of the Heart is loosely based on Henley's family relationships and shares the bittersweet resonance of Williams' *Menagerie* and O'Neill's *Long Day's Journey*. A family play, focused on a particular event that shifts the future for all, was now familiar territory to me. The play is a transparent look at relationships in a troubled family of three daughters in which mother hangs herself and the family cat, making national news. Sixteen years later, as the play opens, youngest daughter Babe shoots her senator husband. All we know about their father, who abandoned the family, is that he had "big white teeth" and that their mother became increasingly depressed and eventually suicidal after he left. Their grandparents, who favored middle daughter, Meg, encouraging her to become a Hollywood star, raised the daughters. Meg, the hard drinking, world-weary sister, now twenty-seven, suffers from overwhelming depression for failing to fulfill her grandfather's dreams of stardom. She has returned home following a psychiatric hospital placement after losing her singing voice. Granddaddy encouraged Babe, age twenty-four, to enter into a loveless marriage with a rich senator in order to gain social status. Babe shoots the senator in his stomach after he walks in on her and her fifteen-year-old lover, Willie Jay. Babe faces jail time for attempted murder and has been recently released on bail by her lawyer, Barnett, who is seeking to avenge his father's mistreatment by Babe's husband. Lenny, the oldest daughter, thirty, has become Granddaddy's caretaker, replacing their grandmother when she died. She is a long-suffering homemaker who has never believed herself worthy of love. Her grandfather has convinced her she will never marry because her shrunken ovaries make her undesirable to men.

In addition to sharing a destructive grandfather and a tragic history of parental abandonment, Lenny, Meg, and Babe have so much in common that we suffer, hope, and become indignant over the injustices committed against them while they struggle through an often unsympathetic, lonely world and unknowingly betray each other. Henley's characters are all damaged, and when they need to rally together to support each other, they are not sure how to do so. One of the strongest features of the script is the history of family wounds that exist in the present. Lenny is still angry Meg got twelve jingle bells on her petticoat while she and Babe only had three a piece. Meg takes a small bite out of every piece of Lenny's birthday assorted crèmes, explaining she was looking for the one with nuts. Lenny is distraught Meg is always taking what isn't hers to take, most notably an old boyfriend that she abandoned who has since married and fathered two children. Meg leaves with him in the evening and does not return until daylight. It was Meg who found their mother dead in the cellar and vividly remembers their father's consistent cruelty to her. As a child, she would look at pictures of people with diseases to prove she could "take it." Still actively self-destructive, Meg lies to their grandfather that she was in a motion picture, made an album, and will be on TV in two weeks. Babe has been physically abused throughout her marriage. She is suicidal, and before shooting her husband, she attempts to shoot herself. Later, in their childhood home, she unsuccessfully tries to hang and asphyxiate herself in the oven. Only Meg's return saves her from these attempts.

Challenges

Clark's set design included a functioning kitchen that was transported into the theater. We were scheduled for a run in the Avery Theater, the performance space inside the Wadsworth Athenaeum. Although it was a magnificent theater, with painted frescos on the ceilings, it was exceeding difficult to unload the unwieldy furniture below ground level. The set included a massive arrangement of authentic wooden cabinets, a real refrigerator with food, an operating sink, a heavy table, front and center, a cot, shelves jammed with props, a saxophone, luggage, a phone, a photo album, and multiple food items used during scenes. Complex costume changes, nuanced lighting, and sound cues were required. We had one weekend to move in. The assistance from the board was exceptional. Cast rehearsal time on location was negligible.

This was the most detailed, realistic set Clark did with me. It is fitting that this family drama takes place in the symbolic hearth of the modern home, the kitchen. The single-set play required a concrete and detailed design.

The show's ending was particularly satisfying. Oldest daughter Lenny celebrates her thirtieth birthday with her sisters, blowing out the candles of her birthday cake and saying, "Just this one moment, and we were all laughing." The spot lighting frames the faces of the women. "Put a Candle in the Window" by Creedence Clearwater Revival plays in the background. A beautifully sharp portrait of the women laughing instantly goes to black, as though the shutter of a camera has frozen the moment.

All the characters are in search of love and commit heartfelt crimes, just as all of us who search for connection are guilty of such crimes. Henley's masterful ability to interweave poignancy and the absurdity makes her a classic playwright. The Masquers, established in 1933, Connecticut's oldest community theater, planned a 2002 season, but it never came to pass. *Crimes of the Heart* was their final production.

Actors

The three sisters need to establish a family history that began in childhood. The early trauma of their mother's suicide and consequential placement with their grandparents—who were critical, unfair, and overly concerned with status—left no opportunity for the sisters to be comforted. As adults, they carry the shame of their mother's suicide, and all are chronically depressed. They do not know how to comfort each other, despite their mutual love for and loyalty to each other. Each woman must appear astonished and confused about what will happen next, and somewhat out of control when events become challenging. Lenny worries and frets, Meg avoids, and Babe disappears into outer space. None of them know what to do and who is in charge. Their deficits in problem solving originate from a lack of the security and identity most people receive from concerned parents. These women are orphans.

Other characters play into this chaos by accommodating the sisters. Each assumes the women are capable of acting on their own behalf. Unfortunately, the sisters need for self-sabotage is greater. The beauty of the play is the recognition that each sister has the other two she can trust. This is a new idea and had evolved from the catalyst of their shared life crisis.

(left to right) Babe (Merri Trout) stands by as Lenny (Robin C'Miel) and Meg (Lori Conley) ponder their predicament regarding their youngest sister's arrest. Set design by Clark Bowlen.

(left to right) Lenny (Robin C'Miel), Babe (Merri Trout), and Meg (Lori Conley) share an intimate moment. Set design by Clark Bowlen.

Clark Bowlen's draft design for the *Crimes of the Heart* set, Mark Twain Masquers, 2001.

CHAPTER 4
COMMUNITY THEATER, 2004 TO 2007

The Mark Twain Masquers had been an exceptionally respectful of our competence, skipping the requisite artistic and technical presentation usually requested by community theater boards. We had access to a private rehearsal space and were given interpretive license, supportive to original work. It was a satisfying experience we looked forward to repeating.

However, it was not until spring 2003 that I found a directing job that attracted my interest. Community theaters typically preselect their season a year in advance. Time is required to apply for the rights to produce the show, and royalties must be paid. If a local company has been granted rights, another cannot produce it at the same time. A director never proposes a script to a company. Therefore, a director with a preference for a particular style must look out for theaters that support that type of show.

A robust community theater group is a self-sustaining organization of diverse artists and support people committed to achieving success. An audition call for such a company draws local talent who expect solid production values, thoughtful directing, and the commitment of fellow actors. Seasonal subscribers are a returning audience who may be encouraged with benefits such as newsletters, free previews, reduced ticket prices, or raffles. Company members, especially board members, are aware and sensitive to the audience's needs and tastes.

A successful community theater is known for producing a certain style of play, technical excellence, good acting and directing, and a consistent quality level throughout the season. Highly efficient companies train participants, including performers, to share technical and other offstage duties such as costuming, props, sound, lighting, and stage management skills. Participants may be police officers, machine operators, teachers, engineers, and students by day, but all find a creative and social outlet in the theater. The group is fluid enough to allow newcomers to enter without disrupting established boundaries, ultimately strengthening the whole.

As a guest director from academic theater I had adjustments to make. The first issue was to understand the limitations of the director role. The rehearsal schedule is limited to hours of operation of the theater rather than the discretion of the director. Blocking changes that diverge from an original script are deferred to the playwright. The board may recommend certain actors not be cast due to temperament, lack of reliability, or other limitations. A director may be told that a certain designer—lighting, set, sound, costume, or other type—will be assigned to the show, and she or he is required to work within those constraints. Clark was no longer my producer. I was assigned a producer. I was sometimes expected to bring my own stage manager to assist me. But I was able to specify that Clark be my designer.

Community theater was an important step in my director development. From the Mark Twain Masquers to The Suffield Players to the New Britain Repertory Company to our collaboration with Connecticut Heritage Productions and The Opera House Players, I learned that companies have various outlooks regarding the value of the artists, about the emphasis on profit margin versus artistic excellence, and about the power balance between company administration and membership.

2004: *The Importance of Being Earnest* by Oscar Wilde

In June 2003, the Suffield Players were searching for a director for *The Importance of Being Earnest*. A community theater in Suffield, Connecticut, with a history of 115 productions, the Suffield Players had the rare distinction of owning their theater. Mapleton Hall was an intimate space in which a core of committed company members shared acting, set building, and production responsibilities. The group was devoted and collaborative. The board was friendly, well informed, and welcoming.

When presenting production concepts to a board, a director proposes an interpretation and design plan. Because I analyze play text before casting, I was able to provide character sketches, themes, script approach, and artistic goals at the interview. Clark's design would accommodate three locations, an apartment, a garden, and a drawing room. This was done with one basic layout, and a variety of furniture pieces. However, Clark would not be my producer or lighting designer, to which we both had to adjust. The result was a less collaborative relationship, which was a loss, but we were grateful to be working together again. When no stage manager could be found, Clark stepped in to assist.

Background

Oscar Wilde was a satirist whose popularity depended on his audience's ignorance of his targets. Although *The Importance of Being Earnest* is in some ways comparable to the drawing-room comedy *She Stoops to Conquer*, Wilde goes further with farce. The outrageous inconsistencies are compounded as the plot progresses, with one difficulty developing because two friends have both assumed the alias "Ernest." Humor is derived from the lack of insight characters reveal when they speak. The one exception to this is Algernon, a hedonistic young man who admits deceiving family and friends to remove himself from unnecessary social obligations. His straight man, Jack, is his best friend, and their relationship is the most honest and developed in the play. Algernon and Jack banter about all manner of social hypocrisy. *Earnest* is entirely dependent on language and the delivery of witty, incongruent lines in nimble, rapid succession. But it is a mistake to interpret Wilde's writing as only parody. His recurrent theme is authenticity versus pretense. This is most apparent in *The Picture of Dorian Gray* in which a handsome man trades eternal youth for an increasingly compromised portrait of his moral character. Wilde's social criticism has a sting. Regrettably, the hypocrisy he was so astute at identifying ultimately triumphed. He was tried and jailed for practicing homosexuality.

Synopsis

The Importance of Being Earnest, with the lightest touch, calls to task a church pastor on his hypocrisy, a grand woman who pretends to have wealth but is actually in debt, an alleged teacher of morality who lost an infant in a train station due to carelessness, and two young women who fall in love with men based on their names. Wilde expresses countless insights into the superficiality of the fashion, dining, drinking, musical, literary, and marital requirements of a society that is self-serving while expressing itself in perfectly polite conversation. The more grandly he does this, the better. Civilized society becomes a thin veneer for the savage attacks young women wage upon each other. Deceit is a daily requirement for young men who create fictional invalids to attend to, which account for otherwise unexplained absences from home. The elders are no better. Lady Bracknell admits lying to her husband and proudly exclaims, "… I do not plan to undeceive him."

Wilde is brilliant at spinning plausible arguments from foolishness. Although the given circumstances are more than unlikely—a baby is switched with a manuscript in a cloak-room—the audience is willing to buy the story, made more outrageous by Lady Bracknell's assumption that her daughter is engaged to a package. The best of today's situation comedies cannot come close to the exquisite wit, timing, and physical clowning opportunities in this script. Although the material was meant to satirize the upper classes who patronized the theater in Wilde's day, his plays were beloved by those he satirized, a tribute to his great skill.

Act 1, in Algernon's apartment, is furnished with rich upholstery and Art Deco style touches and service ware. He is the essence of chic, wearing a wide assortment of smoking jackets and embossed attire. His Aunt Augusta, also classically attired, wears sweeping clothes and tremendously large hats. She is absolutely convinced of her aristocratic status and impressed by wealth. Her daughter Gwendolyn, also fashion conscious, is in love with Algernon's best friend, Jack, who is known to her as Ernest. She confesses that, because of his name, he is the only possible man she could marry. Jack is enchanted by Gwendolyn but repelled by her mother.

Act 2 opens in a sunlit-drenched garden with lush greenery. Delicate patio furniture ornaments the garden where we meet Jack's young ward, Cecily, a terrible student, trying to avoid her German lesson by chattering with her governess, Miss Prism. Reverend Chasuble strolls by, saving Cecily from her studies by taking Miss Prism, his secret love, for a walk. Cecily, alone in the garden, is now free to meet Algernon, who has snuck in to meet her. Jack comes home to find his "brother" planning to stay with him for a long time, judging by his elaborate luggage.

Act 3 brings us into Jack's drawing room, where the confusion is unraveled and, through absolutely ludicrous circumstances, all falls into place for the three couples to be happily matched.

Challenges

Rather than set the play in 1895 Britain, Clark and I decided to move it to 1935 New York City and Westchester County. The American setting, we believed, would make the play more relevant and accessible to our audience. During the Great Depression, as the nation sagged economically, extravagant Hollywood productions with breathtaking starlets in slinky dresses became the national fantasy. *Earnest's* characters, similarly, delude themselves into believing they live in an insular world of possibility and promise. We enhanced things a bit by setting the play when the economic system was on the point of collapse.

Clark planned an elaborate set design, which had to accommodate three settings: Algernon's apartment in Manhattan, the garden of Jack Worthing's manor house in Westchester County, and the drawing room of Jack Worthing's manor house. The basic layout remained the same, with transformations in furniture and lighting. Jerry Zalewski served as lighting designer and did some especially beautiful work in the drawing room in act 3, with shadows of tree branches spilling onto the floor. The interior of the manor house, an elegant and more traditionally furnished room, featured a pastoral scene upstage center. The home had been inherited from Jack's guardian and adoptive father, Mr. Cardew, a wealthy but unpretentious man, who left a fortune to Jack and his granddaughter Cecily. Costuming was beautifully supplied by Suffield's extensive wardrobe storage and some actor additions.

Working with the Suffield Players, a well-organized, well-managed theater group, was an excellent experience for both of us. We were permitted artistic freedom and regarded with kindness and fellowship throughout our assignment. Although we continued to miss aspects of our college theater home, we acknowledged, with gratitude, the opportunity we'd been given to develop our craft.

Actors

Earnest is full of unlikely and impossible situations, which result in a spectacularly joyful conclusion. Although Shakespeare's comedies also end in the reconciliation of estranged lovers, the circumstances are never as absurd as they are in this story. They include an infant switched for a manuscript, best friends leading double lives who discover they are brothers, and use of false identity and later discovery of authenticity. Exaggeration of coincidence is part of Wilde's satiric brilliance and reveals his sense of humor. The play so convincingly engages the audience that each ridiculous revelation is met with audience astonishment and relief.

Since the show addresses pretense, posturing became an important aspect of actor work. Algernon would haughtily pose in his smoking jacket to converse with his servant. Gwendolen fetchingly strikes a model's posture as she announces her requirements for marriage proposal. To make the most of secret alliances, actors mirrored each other's body language. When Algernon and Jack verbally face off in the garden, they also parallel identical aggressive movements. When the women team up to challenge the men, they stand on opposite sides of the stage, in parallel posture. Lady Bracknell, the meddling, socially competitive matriarch, intrusively enters center stage prepared to deliver a dramatic performance. The most important directive for all actors, however, was to play their characters earnestly. Each character must believe his or her viewpoint is right, remaining unaware of contradictions and hypocrisy. To play any Wilde character for laughs diminishes its effectiveness.

(left to right) Gwendolen (Rebecca Meakin) enjoys a cup of tea next to Jack (Shaun Barry) as her mother, Mrs. Bracknell (Jayne Newirth), scowls at her daughter's love interest. Algernon (Thomas Nunes), at home in his Manhattan apartment, finds his aunt's reaction amusing. Set design by Clark Bowlen; lighting by Jerry Zalewski.

(left to right) Merriman (Dana Ring) delivers Algernon's luggage to Jack Worthing's garden and asks where to leave it. Cecily (Rayah Martin) and Algernon (Thomas Nunes) are otherwise engaged. Set design by Clark Bowlen; lighting by Jerry Zalewski.

(left to right) Jack (Shaun Barry) and Algernon (Thomas Nunes) aggressively discuss Algernon's plan to stay with Jack for the next week. Set design by Clark Bowlen; lighting by Jerry Zalewski.

(left to right) Algernon (Thomas Nunes) and Cecily (Rayah Martin) are happily coupled, as Mrs. Brackett sits triumphantly in the drawing room. Reverend Chasuble (Mark Depathy) and Miss Prism (Dorrie Mitchell) have at last revealed their love for each other. Jack, whose Christian name is Ernest, is joyfully paired with Gwendolen (Rebecca Meakin). Set design by Clark Bowlen; lighting by Jerry Zalewski.

2005: *The Rainmaker* by Richard Nash

Background

Clark and I deeply missed the autonomy of executive administration. Unskilled in compliance, and required to leave a situation in which we had thrived, left us feeling confused about where we belonged. Clark had designed dozens of sets for the Repertory Company of New Britain over the decades and enjoyed the collaboration. When a directing slot opened, he suggested I apply and that he would design set and lighting. The show was *The Rainmaker* by Richard Nash, not a brilliant piece of writing, but an acceptable script. Written in 1954, and somewhat dated, it is about a cattle ranch family facing a drought in the western United States, circa 1925.

I applied to the repertory company, presenting script analysis, themes, family relationships, character sketches, artistic vision, and overall message. For the first time, I did not research the life of the playwright. It seemed more relevant for me to determine what I would do with the play than why the playwright wrote the specific story. I argued my strength was successful direction of family plays. Clark presented a design layout to the board, who were already familiar with his work. Although it was not a script I would have selected on my own, it did validate my ability to interpret and create within other's artistic constraints.

Founded in the wake of the Depression, the Repertory Company of New Britain was originally funded as part of a government labor project. The company independently owned their theater. This show was its 230th production.

Synopsis

H. C. Curry, a widower, is the father of three grown children. He is both father and mother to three young adults. His fathering is compassionate, evenhanded and sympathetic. His just interventions with his son, Noah, include censoring the younger man's criticism of his siblings.

Noah is the oldest son; he is extremely responsible and runs the ranch, probably has since he was young. Trained by his father, he has mostly likely improved upon H. C.'s methods. He is hasty in his judgment of others, however. The dispassionate assessment skills that make him such a great businessman are detrimental to his family relationships. Younger brother Jim is, in contrast, vulnerable, warm, and naïve. He says what he feels. He is spontaneous, energetic, and sexual. Their sister, Lizzie, a competent woman, has replaced their mother as the caretaker of the family. Although she yearns for love, she plays it safe rather than risk rejection. She is secretly in love with Deputy File, but assumes it is her role to maintain a home for her father and brothers.

Deputy File, like Lizzie, plays it safe. He longs for a simple home life with someone he loves, but is afraid to take the risk. His first wife left him, and consequently he is afraid to trust again. Sheriff Thomas is the professional equivalent of H. C. Curry. He is a father figure to his deputy. Parallels can be found in both his evenhandedness and benevolence.

Into their lives comes a stranger, Starbuck, who claims to be a miracle worker. This is what makes the play, for me, a parable. Starbuck is a catalyst for others to throw away conventional beliefs and embrace the extraordinary. He is an actor posing as a miracle worker. Unmasked, he is a lonely dreamer, who admits dreaming is better than living. Lizzie is able to give him absolution by seeing his goodness. He is able to see her beauty. He is both the miracle worker and the miracle. He claims to be a rainmaker, a magician who fulfills dreams people have abandoned.

The play is about transformation. Although it is called a "romantic comedy," I found it to be a spiritual play about the restoration of hope. A plain sister transforms into a beautiful woman. An older know-it-all brother softens. A younger brother with low self-esteem discovers confidence. The Curry father, in his fifties, pretends to think rain may be magically manifested. The fantasy of creating a fresh situation from a demoralizing one appeals to him. He takes Starbuck's offer, not because he believes him, but because he is buying hope for his family to think outside boundaries of their self-limiting assumptions.

Starbuck is the catalyst for family transformation. Like the Great Oz, the magic he delivers each person is the opportunity to see himself or herself honestly. Family members are given assignments particularly suited to challenge their limiting self-images. A mule kicks Noah after he is directed by Starbuck to tie its hind legs together. Jim is told to beat a giant drum when he gets the urge, reinforcing his self-confidence. H. C. Curry paints a white arrow of Starbuck's specially formulated mix away from the house so lightning doesn't strike it, and, in the process, paints himself white. Daughter Lizzie transforms into a beautiful woman when Starbuck falls in love with her. Meanwhile, her unexpressed interest in File and his in her is put to a test. Starbuck's attentiveness has made her feel desirable. File expresses his true feelings for her, and Lizzie, emboldened by Starbuck, may now accept File's love. Starbuck's character shifts from con man to creator. He becomes a savior figure, not by performing magic, but by helping each person see into his or her heart. As this transformation occurs, Starbuck is transformed. Thus, by act 3, the initially fast-talking Starbuck of act 1 has become honest with himself. He takes the whole family with him, and the family, in turn, inspires him to self-honesty. The emotional climate of the family is restored. The symbolic drought of fixed ideas is now cleansed by nature's rain, which erupts from the sky in a giant thunderstorm.

Challenges

Clark's set design, true to style, was one of open interiors, with defining space of stairs, front door, and window. Downstage right, the sheriff's office, with desk and cot, was a separate area. The tack room, in which Starbuck and Lizzie meet, is located stage left. Center stage and most of the playing area was devoted to the family kitchen. Daytime lighting was harsh and aggressive, suggesting relentless heat. A pan of water sat in the sink, which family members would dip cloths into to cool the back of their necks and palms. The men had T-shirt tans, wore farmer's hats, had patches of sweat across their backs, and carried kerchiefs to dab sweat. A small, ineffective fan whirled on the kitchen counter. The action of the play, in three acts, takes place in daytime, evening, and later the same night. Part of the lighting concept was to have a dramatically shifting sky that grew darker and darker, finally bursting into lightning and pouring great sheets of rain down at the finale of the show. Although Clark designed the lighting scheme for the show, he did not operate the board, and the subtle shifting of light from day to twilight to evening to night was unfortunately lost in board operation. I did call several technical meetings to correct these imbalances, but to our disappointment, they were ignored.

Actors

Once again addressing family structure, my instinct was to discover the dynamics of how the group worked. Noah, the eldest, feels his father fails to communicate the hardships of life. His mission is to temper his father's optimism with a dose of harsh reality. Noah's rudeness compensates for what he thinks are failings of their father. In reality, he bullies his brother, and to a lesser extent, his sister, and is unkind to his father. Youngest brother Jim is the target of Noah's criticism, receiving Noah's overbearing parental comments with resentment and helplessness.

Lizzie and her father have an alliance that protects her from Noah's intervention, from which she remains detached. She loves all three men with equal loyalty and doesn't play them against each other. These relationship patterns were discovered, as usual, with age regression and family improvisation to clarify their early roots. Both Noah and Lizzie have assumed adult responsibilities at an early age, which leave them prematurely grown-up but also longing for the love and understanding that they missed as children. The best aspect of this cast was the vulnerability the actors displayed in trusting the unfulfilled yearning of their characters.

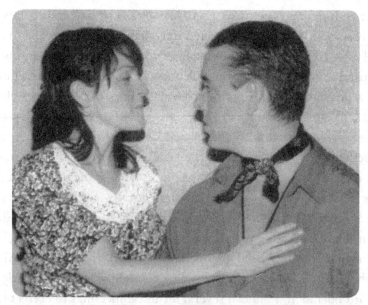

Lizzie (Cheryl Guertin) gazes at Starbuck (Joe Archibald) as he tries to convince her she is beautiful. Set design by Clark Bowlen; lighting by Michael Bane.

Clark Bowlen's set design for *The Rainmaker* at New Britain Repertory, 2005.

2006: *Jacques Brel Is Alive and Well in Paris,* Narrative Adaptation by K. Keena

Background

In 2006, Herman Shemonsky, professional actor, director, singer and long-time friend, proposed collaborating with us for a Jacques Brel revival. Clark and I were hesitant; the only musical we had produced was *Came So Far for Beauty*, featuring the words and music of Leonard Cohen. Herman suggested he and I codirect and Clark produce. I knew from the Cohen production that the music would need as much rehearsal time as the acting. If we were to do another, I wanted to rehearse with the musical director to integrate both seamlessly as we proceeded. Serendipitously, the perfect pianist arrived, applying for musical director. If it had not been for her expertise, the program would never have become the success it was.

The MCC theater program had ended in 2001, although Clark remained a tenured professor. Consequently, we needed an organization to sponsor us. Steve Starger, who was working in the noncredit division as the advisor to MCC's Older Adult Association, gave us an excellent referral to the college administration. Many group members had seen our previous productions and agreed as an organization to sponsor the project.

As is my practice, I researched Brel's life, discovering he had been a cabaret singer in Nazi-occupied Brussels for four years. I reviewed the original US production by Eric Blau and Mort Shuman in the 1960s. Meanwhile, Clark located photographs of Brel to use in overhead slide projections, concretely assuring the musician's presence on stage.

Synopsis

Listening to the themes from the American production, I envisioned Brel's struggles and constraints within a restrictive society. I proposed that the show would have more resonance against a socio-political backdrop as the story of an artist who refused to be silent in a genocidal regime. Brel's personal history had been absent from the original musical, and I recommended a more socially inclusive narration to make the show our own. His later songs, about a soldier's loss of identity, the horrors of slaughter, and the pressures to conform, certainly have greater impact when viewed as atrocities committed in Nazi-occupied Brussels. Historic events would parallel Brel's journey from childhood and innocence through early adulthood, love, heartbreak, disillusionment, cynicism, horror, and despair to compassion, resilience, gratitude, and hope.

Our company of eight was comprised of four males, two females plus our female pianist, who occasionally sang and acted, and a male narrator, who sang two numbers. For each number selected, I designed a performance concept that would bring the song to life, either in dance or drama. The song "Carousel," for example, was dramatized as actors twirled, facing the audience, while moving up and down to create the effect of riding a carousel. As each actor advances closer to the audience, his or her voice becomes louder. The song "Next!" describes the anonymity of army enlistment dramatized by male actors standing in line, relinquishing individual differences such as hairstyles, clothing, mannerisms, etc.

The show was divided into two acts, featuring twenty-two numbers, progressively expressing deepening emotional and moral struggles.

Herman coached the actors to integrate dramatic work with musical clarity and projection. My initial blocking concepts were improved by his enhanced direction. In addition to his magnificent narrative delivery, he sang "If You Go Away" and "If We Only Have Love," two of the production's most stirring songs.

Challenges

My task was to tell the story of each song as originally as possible. Clark and I shared a bias that musicals often feature actors whose work is self-conscious, showy, and contrived. We were interested in organic continuity. The college had undergone major renovations and the small, intimate theater where we'd staged prior productions was no longer available. Instead, a lecture-hall-size auditorium with a raised stage would be our performance space. Hoping to shrink the expanse, we arranged bar stools in horseshoe pattern facing the audience. In addition, we drew the curtains by one panel stage left and right to create a more intimate setting. When the actors were not performing a number, they returned to their respective seats and observed the scenes, emotionally engaged in the action.

Company involvement was as inclusive as possible. Whenever the entire group could participate in a number, they did. Particular songs needed to be solo, but were enhanced by backup singers or additional characters. Couples sung love songs to each other. Several ballads were danced. One arrangement was staged as a barbershop quartet. Songs about military service were staged as warfare or drill scenes. It was important to vary pace and subject to sustain audience interest. The narrator device to historically and personally link events gave the show a broader dimension and appeal. As a nonchoreographer, I muddled through dance configurations I'd conceptually described, and actors practiced while I directed them to modify particular aspects. The final number, "If We Only Have Love," concluded with the audience using American Sign Language to join the cast in celebration of Brel's courage and art. Since the audience was not deaf, we included sign-language symbols and words in the program and also had actors direct the audience in the signing of each word. The result was a beautiful silent moment of unity with Brel.

Actors

Herman, understandably, was concerned about the quality of the performers' voices. I wanted to be sure the acting was strong. Musical director Jessica Martinik agreed to work with performers outside scheduled rehearsals, which allowed us to place maximum emphasis on production values.

Codirecting presented particular challenges to us and also to the actors. Herman and I were in agreement artistically and operationally. When he was unable to attend rehearsals, however, actors became understandably confused. I would direct a segment that Herman might later rearrange. This was not difficult for me, but frustrating for actors. I was asked whether my authority ultimately carried more weight than Herman's. I realized that Clark and I had the advantage of going home together and reviewing the minutiae of a rehearsal for hours. At the next rehearsal, we would present a united, thoroughly developed solution to potential conflicts. Herman and I had no such luxury. His commute was formidable, and he had other responsibilities. For cast cohesion, it would have been beneficial if only one of us had final artistic approval.

Narrative Creation

It is unnecessary for a director to be a writer or playwright. It is, in fact, unusual. I happened fall into these circumstances, which brought added dimension to projects. It was interesting for Clark, Steve, and me to imagine possibilities outside the existing framework. For us, it became more about who we were than something we had to do, an approach we found rewarding. This creative environment led me to develop the Brel narrative. As a director, I have a natural inclination to associate diverse themes and blend them into an original work.

For those who are interested in a closer examination, the entire Brel text may be found in the appendix.

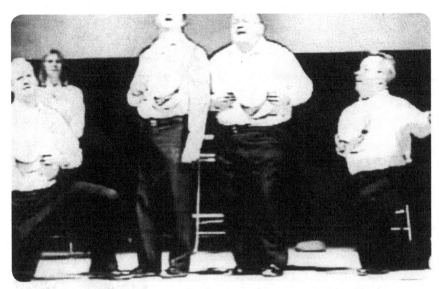

(left to right) Company members Eric Prause, Dana Ring, Dana O'Neal, and Tony Enright sing "Madeleine" as a barbershop quartet. Lighting and set design by Clark Bowlen.

Narrator Herman Shemonsky sings a moving rendition of "If You Go Away." Lighting and set design by Clark Bowlen.

Eric Prause (right) sings the story of his love, "Fanette," danced by Dorrie Mitchell (left) as the ensemble listens. Lighting and set design by Clark Bowlen.

Jessica Martinik, pianist, plays as cast sings "Brussels," about the liveliness in the city. Lighting and set design by Clark Bowlen.

Company members sing "Carousel" as they move up and down and circle around, becoming the carousel. Lighting and set design by Clark Bowlen.

2007: *Pvt. Wars* by James McLure

Background

Jacques Brel had been a positive experience for Clark and me. Unfortunately, directing opportunities at Repertory Theatre Company of New Britain were slow to develop, although I continued to work diligently as a board member. Energized by independent work, we were ready to begin another project. Since *Brel* had, to some extent, mended our artistic estrangement from the college, we realized we could continue productions with sponsorship. Because we were independent artists, the college could not prevent our collaboration.

Brel's proceeds had been donated to the Older Adults Association and the MCC French club. If we could find a deserving college program, we could offer to fundraise in exchange for sponsorship. We thought of veterans almost immediately. *Who By Fire* had been an empowering project for all involved, satisfying our artistic and humanitarian longings. Clark contacted the veterans advisor at the college, proposing a fundraiser. The project would raise textbook money for student veterans who could not otherwise purchase them. The Liberal Arts Division joined the sponsorship.

Synopsis

James McLure, author of our 1999 show *Lone Star/Laundry and Bourbon*, about one Vietnam veteran's readjustment difficulties, wrote *Pvt. Wars*. The story concerns three Vietnam veterans of diverse backgrounds. Natwick, an overeducated and over privileged misfit from Long Island, joined the service to escape family pressures. Silvio, an Italian American street punk with violent tendencies and impulse control issues, is chronically agitated. He continues to see himself as a ladies' man although his genitals were lost in-country. Gately, traumatically brain injured, struggles with abstract ideas and cannot express himself or recall his married life, despite a visit from his wife.

Within the service, various assignments carry different levels of status for veterans. The deciding issues are the level and frequency of risk in the line of duty. Frontline, boots-on-the-ground grunts (marines) rank highest for courage in Vietnam, having faced the heaviest fire, casualties, most frequent ambushes, and most gruesome assignments. Silvio, a frontline warrior, has paid the greatest price for his bravery. He is aware of the others' active-duty assignments and resents Natwick, who was combat support. Gately, also frontline, has paid dearly, too, but is unconcerned about status and sees people as equals. Despite Natwick's position in the rear, he sustained injuries and must wear a permanent catheter strapped to his leg. Silvio shows him no mercy, relentlessly taunting him. Gately is easy to manipulate and influence and idolizes Silvio. All three talk about their ability to leave "any time," but it is clear no one is ready to face life outside hospital walls. Gately, although mentally impaired, has a great depth of feeling and the most access to his emotions. He is able to cry easily and also experience joy.

In the play, brief snapshots illustrate particular moments in the men's daily lives. This device creates the sense of time passing and suggests the hours of boredom and loneliness the men experience between encounters.

Challenges

Pvt. Wars depends on the actors performing on an essentially bare stage. Only a generic card table, several plastic chairs, and a vinyl sofa suggest the hospital. This focuses all attention on character development. It is a show in which each person evolves and is affected by his interactions with the other two characters. Lighting played a critical part in the production, with shifts defining mood. Natwick's suicide attempt was lit in a foreboding red. A multicolored dawn greets Silvio as he reads his sister's letter telling him he cannot move back home. Flashbacks; sounds of fitful, troubled sleep; and sudden unprovoked bursts of anger dominate the performances. A particularly delicate challenge for the director is the balance between the comic dialogue and the tragic circumstances of the situation. When played effectively, the show is tremendously poignant.

Actors

We were fortunate to cast military veterans for all three roles, which established an immediate rapport between the actors. They understood feelings of suppressed identity, ambivalence toward authority, and abandonment, if not personally, then through connection with other veterans. Working with veterans is similar to ensemble work. There is a common language, experience, and implicit trust that, in other circumstances, would take years to build. The comradeship and esprit de corps bypass potential upstaging and personal disagreements, facilitating teamwork. No other group has such mutual regard and sensitivity to fellow actors. When your lives depend on one another, cooperation and resilience are everything.

This personal alliance worked very well against the backdrop of alienation the script explores. Three veterans have become so entrenched in their private wars that their connection to each other is impaired. Yet their only hopes for reconnection are with each other. Without family, without professional identity, returning from war with lifelong impairments, they must adapt to a world that is indifferent to their suffering.

(left to right) Cedric Johnson as Natwick, Dana O'Neal as
Gately, and Phil Godeck as Silvio celebrate Silvio's hospital
release. Lighting and set design by Clark Bowlen.

2007: *Italian American Reconciliation* by John Patrick Shanley

Background

I had suggested directing John Patrick Shanley's *Italian American Reconciliation* for a September 2007 opening at the Repertory Theatre Company of New Britain. My fellow board members agreed. Shanley had written *Moonstruck*, the much-loved film featuring Cher and Nicolas Cage. In both scripts, his characters are working-class Italian Americans who, although inarticulate in their deepest longings, are emotionally passionate individuals. Clark was my set designer and technical director. I was challenged by the work, which was different from the other shows I had directed, mainly because the characters could not express themselves verbally.

Synopsis

Shanley calls his work a "folktale," and *Italian American* represents the multigenerational ethnic community where members share cultural customs. Old World principles, such as men as the undisputed heads of households, are presumed. Little Italy is an insular world apart from greater New York. Much is made of a man needing machismo to guide his family wisely. The structure of the play has the character Aldo introduce himself from the audience and subsequently step into the story to reenact his friend's marital problems. He frames his goal as wanting to teach the audience. The lesson has to do with losing the ability to love and losing yourself in the process. He dramatizes this through his friend Huey's story.

Huey Maximilian Bonfiglio is in an impossible dilemma; he believes he left his virility with his ex-wife. After two years of divorce, it is now time for him to reclaim his power. When we meet him, he wears a poet's white shirt with billowing sleeves, jodhpurs, and embossed royal blue slippers. It is clear to Aldo that Huey is losing his sanity. Huey reads a poorly written poem full of anger and bitterness in which he devalues himself. He asks Aldo an outrageous favor: to "soften up" his ex-wife Janice so she'll be in the mood for his latest overtures. Huey suggests Aldo do so through a sexual encounter. Narrator Aldo is a streetwise, fast-talking guy who is short in stature, but big on personality. He wants to be respected and loved. He embellishes stories to make them more attractive. Unfortunately for him, every time he tries to be smooth, he turns into an unwitting clown. However, he is a true friend to Huey, his best friend, who lacks his self-confidence. Huey relies on for Aldo for advice, although whether his heartfelt suggestions have merit is another story.

Huey disappointed Janice because he did not "take charge" in their marriage. She abused him, and he accepted the abuse, which includes shooting his dog. She is a passionate character and hopes to instigate a confrontation through her unacceptable behaviors. Aldo has a message for the audience: when a man goes to reconcile with his wife, he is dying because he's refused to live. His conclusion is that "the great, the only success, is to be able to love." Huey confronts Janice, expressing his authentic feelings about her abusive behavior. She responds with gratitude.

Challenges

The beauty of this script is the disparity between the depth of feeling within the characters and their ability to express those feelings. This creates many comic moments, but the comedy is a byproduct of poignancy. Shanley's gift for creating distinct characters gives a director a rich opportunity to develop individual idiosyncrasies. Each character is missing something that is within his or her grasp if habitual attitudes can be surrendered. Meanwhile, misinterpretation is common. Advice from third parties is the preferred problem-solving approach, compounding confusion.

The set design is similar in concept to that of *The Glass Menagerie*. Narrator Aldo, like Tom, stands outside the set, which he has arranged to dramatize his tale. Afterward, he steps into the story as a character. Three different locations define the set. Each is a consciously distinct playing area meant to look as though Aldo has mapped out locations to facilitate his story. Center stage is Huey's apartment, full of stacked, unpacked boxes. Stage right is Janice's balcony—floral, romantic, and Romeo/Juliet-like, with patio chairs and garden below. Pop's Soup Kitchen functions as a community meeting place, a gloomy half-lit diner with a back-wall mural of Roman ruins.

The Mark Twain Masquers and the Suffield Players had technical crews on hand to assemble the set. At New Britain Repertory, no such crew was available. Clark and I and a few devoted actors completed set construction. Several board members joined us during the process, but the company was not organized to accommodate set building. Standard protocol was for directors furnish their own construction crews. It hadn't been a problem with *Rainmaker* because the set design required minimal assembly. *Italian American* required a two-story structure, including a stairway and balcony. The soup kitchen required a countertop with the capacity for food service. Nevertheless, we persevered, and the show went on as scheduled. The music was especially wonderful and enhanced both the male/female romantic roles with heightened, unrealistic passion. Numbers such as "O Solo Mia," "Papa Loves to Mambo," "Turandot," "The Summer Wind" and "Come Back to Sorrento" added to the atmosphere of this comedy/drama.

Actors

The actor playing Huey had never been onstage. I met him at Costco and recruited him after deciding no one else could do justice to the role. His raw honesty and vulnerability required no coaching. The disadvantage of having an inexperienced actor in a leading role is that the individual is somewhat of a wild card, having never performed on a live stage. We met for additional line rehearsals in which he learned to paraphrase prior to memorizing precise dialogue. This technique is helpful to new actors, and I'd used it with positive results when working with veterans. His counterpart, in the role of Aldo, was an experienced actor who was well prepared for each rehearsal. Although the resulting imbalance was difficult to manage, I was confident we had the right cast and remained so throughout the run. All the characters required actors with a type of raw honesty that is without delicacy. People blurt out their truest feelings, even when doing so sounds desperate, manic, or worse. The roller coaster of emotions exceeds characters' ability to manage these feelings. The cast delivered this quality to each performance, creating immediacy to every moment. The play includes grown men reciting poetry, ex-wives firing guns, and best friends agreeing to seduce ex-wives. Their struggles are no different than any of ours, but the precision with which Shanley defines the culture makes it both specific and universal.

Beyond Community Theater

During the rehearsal and the run of the show, my original directing mentor and dearest friend Barbara Kennedy lay dying of a brain tumor in a Boston hospital. Her diagnosis and death were mere months apart. During that time, the board member who usually cleaned the bathrooms and picked up the theater after performances refused to do so for the run of *Italian American Reconciliation*, threatening to shut the show down unless someone else took over that responsibility. I volunteered when it became obvious no one else would. This commitment prevented me from visiting my dying friend for three consecutive weekends.

In addition, a disagreement had resulted in one distraught member rushing out of a board meeting. As a therapist, I knew the first rule for group work is for people in conflict to remain in the room until a resolution is reached. For Clark and me, the joy of theater is derived from the collaboration with fellow artists and comradeship of working together on a project. I was a board member and director for the company, yet I wasn't trusted with the key to open wardrobe storage.

However, it was the selection of a musical director for the 2007–8 production *Blues in the Night* that ended our service. Suffice it to say that an internal disagreement brought group dysfunction center stage. It was late fall, early winter of 2007. As my dear friend lived her final days, I had no tolerance for in-fighting or wasting time doing anything other than artistic work. I quit the board, and Clark quit with me. It was fortunate we did. He was only years away from the end of his life when we decided to establish our own theater company.

Repertory Theatre of New Britain
23 Norden Street, New Britain, CT

$62nd$
Season

 Italian

By John
Patrick
Shanley

American

Tony and Pulitzer winner.
Author of MOONSTRUCK

Directed by Kathleen Keena

Reconciliation

A Folk Tale Comedy

Sept 14-15, 21-23, 28-29, 2007

Friday-Saturday 8:15p.m. Sunday 5:15p.m.

Adults $18 • Seniors/Students $15 • Children 12 and under $10
Group Rates 20 or more $13

Tickets: 860-223-3147
or www.nbrep.org

Supported in part by
United Arts 2005-2006

CONNECTICUT

Connecticut Commission
on Culture & Tourism

Poster for *Italian American Reconciliation* featuring photos of
(top to bottom) Phil Godeck as Aldo, Arty Hendrick, as Huey
and Alena Cybart as Janice. Set design by Clark Bowlen.

CHAPTER 5
INDEPENDENT THEATER, 2008 TO 2012

Our greatest artistic fulfillment was the founding of our own organization, the Veterans Memorial Theater Company (VMTC). Combining interests in social relevance with empowerment of neglected populations via theater, we gathered an interested group of military veterans. Community theater work convinced us that although we could produce any style of play, we preferred working in the realm of social responsibility. It was purposeful and satisfying. The death of my thirty-five-year-old brother and my uncle, both military veterans, in a private plane crash in 1991 had initiated our work with veterans. Clark and I knew quite a few actors who were military veterans. We also ran audition notices in the local city papers, stressing that no stage experience was required to join the company. I followed leads from the Veterans Education Project, veterans centers, and college veterans support services. Veterans are especially prevalent in social service professions such as education, government, and public or civil service. Many return to employment as skilled laborers and pursue their service-oriented careers.

Clark had ended his full-time career at the college as emeritus professor of communications, but decided to continue teaching one acting course per semester. I had been on disability due to multiple sclerosis for five years. Both of us had been waiting to work together again without other commitments to distract us. Our spirits were high, and our founding members were a diverse group of talented veterans. As a group, we composed a mission statement. We determined that we needed to apply for nonprofit status. As an organization, we would require bylaws, a board of directors, and officers of the board. We spent from January to June 2008, drafting and finalizing the documents that would be the underpinnings of the organization. We never doubted we would accomplish our goals despite the economic crash that followed, the escalation of US military involvement in the Middle East, and the vast unemployment that crippled the country as the market collapsed. Our timing for opening a new theater company could not have been worse.

Specific difficulties unique to veterans' theater include general public apathy about the psychological damage of warfare. Theater brings the abstract into the personal. It promotes identification with characters. Theater evokes empathy and causes us to more deeply experience our humanity. Such insights create feelings of responsibility that are often difficult for civilians to bear. In addition, veterans, although positive about the company and its productions, often preferred to donate money rather than attend our shows, wanting to avoid the pain of stimulating their own memories. Consequently, our target audience often stayed at home during performances. We slowly and painfully acquired these lessons over the years. Nevertheless, for those who did participate, it was generally a cathartic, healing experience.

It is not unusual for veterans to avoid disclosing their service history. There are three significant reasons for this response.

1. Memories are painful and private and open up sensory details in disturbing intensity.
2. Warfare is unfathomable to civilians and futile to share.
3. Identifying oneself as a veteran may trigger suppressed rage and depression that has been compartmentalized to facilitate daily functioning.

It therefore was imperative for each member to decide his or her appropriate level of involvement with the company and to have the freedom to modify the commitment if it becomes detrimental. We also had to find veterans who were mentally and emotionally resilient enough to discuss topics such as postwar adjustment and re-assimilation, betrayal, and grief and to dramatize them on stage. That required trust, self-confidence, and emotional stability—attributes needed to create a believable role in performance. Veterans' theater work is a call to the exceptional. From the revival production of *Pvt. Wars* through to a company fundraiser, a full-scale musical, an original drama, and an updated edition of *Who By Fire*, the company persevered. Changes in board membership, increasingly challenging productions, the relevance of our work as well as Clark's progressive illness, incapacitation, and impending death engendered a deeply determined group commitment. Our model of a healthy, functional theater group was finally realized.

2008: *Pvt. Wars* (Revival) by James McLure

Background

Developing the VMTC board came about as a byproduct of our organizational work. Phil Godeck emerged as group leader and was nominated president of the company. His promotion of our mission to other theater companies, the media, and the public was responsible for our community growth. I was nominated artistic director while Clark was vice president and treasurer. I carried the office of secretary for the first year by default. Steve Starger became playwright, musical director, coproducer, and artistic advisor for all projects. Frank Bradley, who had also left the Repertory Theater of New Britain after decades, became PR chair. Herman Shemonsky, who we hoped would direct the musical *Blues in the Night* for the Rep in collaboration with Steve, became our administration officer. Other founding members included Hartford Green Party activist Dave Ionno, author Ron Winter, and the multitalented actor Dana O'Neal.

During the six months that the company was forming, Clark and I had corresponded with *New York Times* bestselling editor Andrew Carroll for rights to selected letters from his 2001 book, *Letters Home*. The glitch was that it was going to be made into a movie, and we had to use letters that would not be reproduced on film. The letters spanned the Civil War, World Wars I and II, Korea, Cold War, Vietnam, Persian Gulf, Somalia, and Bosnia. From soldiers to doctors to family members to heads of state, the sample was exhaustive and touched many humanitarian themes.

After six months of uncertainty, Phil suggested that we revisit *Pvt. Wars* (see chapter 4). It had been two years since our show, but if Dana and Phil were willing, it could be rehearsed with minimal hours. In addition, it was a show of proven success. Phil reached out to Connecticut Heritage Productions about a collaboration. The company had an opening in its season if we were willing to share the expenses and gate. Its small grant would help with publicity and programs, and we would need to rent theater space and assign tech. Clark, Phil, and I met with Peter Loffredo, artistic director and president of Connecticut Heritage Productions, and drew up an agreement. It was a wise choice. Because Clark and I had previously produced it, we knew what it required. Although Cedric Johnson could not join the cast as Natwick, Foster Reese stepped in and crafted a finely nuanced character, quite the equal to Phil's Silvio and Dana's Gately. The collaboration was mutually advantageous for both companies and an artistic success.

Synopsis

As director, I was interested in going deeper into the script to develop the darker psychological damage within each man. Each actor created a backstory prior to his character's service and VA hospital admission. Silvio is in love with his sister and filled with the rage of repressing his feelings. He overcompensates by becoming a ladies' man, but since the loss of his genitals has become violent and psychotic. Dana O'Neal created Gately as a military radio operator who accidentally caused the death of his fellow crewmates. Rather than face this memory, he has disassociated from his prior life. Instead, his obsession with radios is his way of attempting to correct his terrible crime. Natwick, secretly terrified he has no writing talent, is addicted to sarcasm to cover his fear of being ordinary when his family demands excellence. The additional emphasis on personality issues made the characters more troubled, needy, and real. In this version of the play, trust issues were deeper, the feelings of abandonment by country and family were sharper, and the ability to listen and reach out to each other more tentative and risky.

Despite their fears, however, each character is haunted by a desperate need to connect with the others. Each is trapped inside his own "private war," which keeps him emotionally frozen. The beauty of the script is that the brief scenes describe transformative moments that shift the static nature of each character, opening up windows of opportunity so each can recognize he is being cared for and heard in a new way. For Silvio, it is a moment of murderous rage directed at Natwick, locking him in a chokehold at knifepoint before recognizing his mistake. When Natwick pleads for his life, Silvio comes to his senses, realizing where he is and whom he is attacking. Natwick, albeit gradually, recognizes the folly of his mean-spirited sarcasm, which is directed at Silvio. He recognizes the extent of Silvio's emotional wounds. He intentionally softens his approach, although Silvio misreads his first attempts at friendship as sexual overtures.

The most amazing breakthrough, however, is that of Gately, who has a traumatic brain injury (TBI). He has been fixing radios since the start of the play, but unknown to him, both Silvio and Natwick steal the parts so he can't complete the repairs. At Silvio's going home party, Gately announces the radio is fixed. Natwick picks the radio up, in a gesture to throw it away, and it suddenly broadcasts a military march. The men reassure him he will now be able to go home, too. Gately, who has up to this point been speaking in a TBI-halting drawl, begins to speak fluently and coherently about his father, recovering his higher functioning. Although this is not specifically stated in the script, we discovered as much in rehearsal and followed it to the end of the play. Our assumption was that the repair of the radio had restored some pretrauma performance just as the radio failure had caused the regression of his intellect when his brothers-in-arms lost their lives.

Before morning dawns, Silvio discovers he isn't leaving the VA hospital because his sister can't take him home. The three veterans will continue to live together. But what is different is that a fragile connection of trust and friendship has been made and, for the first time, each has felt the support of the others. Their overtures are less than ideal, granted. But this is a story about veterans.

Challenges

The deeper psychological exploration required more from all of us. This time we worked on subtext, instead of focusing on comic timing, which is certainly an aspect, especially for first half of the show. Each actor focused internally on what was not being said. This approach led us to a very different interior dialogues and characterizations. Revisiting a play I'd already produced was a challenge I had not looked forward to. In retrospect, I discovered that fresh discoveries can be made and new levels of insight mined in a well-written play.

Actors

In one scene, Gately recounts a recent visit from his wife to Silvio. Although he does not remember his marriage, he does recall her name. She tells him to come home and asks for a kiss. Gately tells Silvio he couldn't remember how to kiss. His next line is, "Isn't that funny?" Dana O'Neal, who was playing Gately, was throwing the line away as if it were a casual comment. It felt wrong to me, and I eventually stopped him. We discussed Gately's grief at the loss of his past life. Playing the scene with the motivation of expressing grief to Silvio changed the tone of the scene. Gately describes his wife's visit to confess his mental deficits and be understood. By the time Dana delivered the tag line, he was sobbing. The scene made sense.

Many scenes came to life when we dove into the emotional content behind seemingly insignificant banter. In one scene, Natwick attempts suicide. He is troubled that Gately and Silvio have gone out to pick up girls and didn't invite him. He observes that they are his closest friends and don't even like him. On the surface, this is funny. On closer examination, it is a reason for suicide. He is unloved and unlovable. All three characters must project this alienating wound. They are the abandoned casualties of war, now institutionalized. Their redemption will be found in trusting and being trustworthy in relationship with each other.

(left to right) Natwick (Foster Reese) pouts after Gately (Dana O'Neal) shows Silvio (Phil Godeck) his Duke Snider card, but Silvio refuses to pass it to Natwick. Lighting and set design by Clark Bowlen.

(left to right) Natwick (Foster Reese) is wary of Silvio's (Phil Godeck) constant criticism. Gately (Dana O'Neal) looks on. Lighting and set design by Clark Bowlen.

(left to right) Gately (Dana O'Neal) fixes a radio as Silvio (Phil
Godeck) jots down notes concerning who's who in the VA
hospital. Lighting and set design by Clark Bowlen.

2009: *American Warriors: Scenes from Twentieth-Century War Scripts*

Background

By this time, Clark had been diagnosed with the terminal illness
multiple systems atrophy, which shuts down autonomic nervous system
functioning. His early symptoms were balance difficulties, weakness,
exhaustion, and loss of concentration and memory. However, it was not
yet apparent how ravaging the disease would become, and we were both
more comfortable dealing with the present.

Steve had offered to write a full-length show for VMTC to premiere
in winter 2009. Due to theater location complications, we were compelled
to postpone the production despite an extended search for sites. Once
again, Phil suggested an alternative that solved several problems
simultaneously. He proposed a fundraiser that could be presented in any
high school or community auditorium: if we featured war-related scenes

by contemporary playwrights, we could put up a show demonstrating our strengths. These included military veterans as actors, a naturalistic style of performance, and accurate historical references and costuming. As we discussed the concept, our production format ultimately evolved into play selections from World War I, World War II, Korea, Vietnam, and Iraq. Author Ronald Winter volunteered to give a slide presentation that addressed topics from his book *Masters of the Art: A Fighting Marine's Memoir of Vietnam*. Steve Starger would coordinate music representative of each era to introduce scenes.

Synopsis

While searching veterans web posts, I came across a particularly poignant entry by Major Andrew Olmsted, which had been published after his death in January 2008 while he was on assignment in Iraq. In it, he addresses his reasons for choosing military service. I suggested to Steve that Major Olmsted would be a powerful counterpoint to his play, *Slick Sleeves*. Steve incorporated Olmsted as a commentator on the action. Our fundraiser opened with veteran Frank Schiavone playing the major. His unapologetic performance set a dignified yet challenging tone to the evening as he related his struggles over why the military exists, why he serves, and how his views of life and death dispelled romantic notions of soldier service.

Following this performance, we presented a scene from British playwright R. C. Sheriff's *Journey's End* that dramatized the stress of World War I trench warfare. Captain Stanhope has been serving at the front for several years, long enough to require daily intoxication. But no matter how much he drinks, some memories just don't go away. That's why he refuses to give his second lieutenant a break. An altercation ensues, and the junior officer is ordered into combat despite his personal objections.

To dramatize World War II, Phil played both Joe Keller and his son Chris in Arthur Miller's *All My Sons*. Joe authorized the welding of faulty cylinder heads of air force P-40s, and his son led the company that perished due to his father's negligence. The Korean War–era *The Brig* is performed in a confrontational, in-your-face performance style. Al Terry worked directly with audience members, addressing them at their tables as if they were marine prisoners. Elizabeth Reynolds played a strategic intelligence officer in Vietnam from *A Piece of My Heart*, prevented from delivering information pertinent to the Tet Offensive to senior officers. Finally, US Marine door gunner and author Ron Winter discussed his missions in Vietnam, fighting enemy troops and rescuing the wounded during hostile fire.

Challenges

Steve had contacted Adath Israel Synagogue in Middletown, which agreed to host our event. However, we only had several weeks to put the show together. Although scene selection was not difficult, casting was somewhat pressured. I arranged individual rehearsal times for each actor in our home, which kept me busy. Clark's neurological brain disease compromised him, and his mobility was limited. He walked haltingly and with a cane. Our company was scheduled for only one dress rehearsal prior to performance, and the cast had never seen each other's work. The show coordination would require rapid blocking of entrances and exits, timed with music and lights, in one evening. It was an unthinkable proposal if we had considered the shows' demands. By this time, however, Clark and I felt that artistic creation was the easy part. We had the theater space, we had the actor talent, and would present a worthwhile show.

Actors

Phil, VMTC's president, and I, artistic director, introduced the organization's mission and production to the actors. Despite the downturn in the economy, we were committed to pursuing our goal to give voice to veterans. We defined ourselves as a company for veterans. All group members worked with particular diligence to become a team, despite the limited time we had to do so. All of the presentations, except one, were individual performances. Yet the company functioned with solidarity that became the hallmark of our identity. Clark displayed gracious dignity, and no one could tell how seriously ill he was.

Major Olmstead (Frank Schiavone) explains why he selected a military career.

Captain Stanhope (Ben Pitz) listens to Second Lieutenant
Hibbert (Rick Briercheck) request a leave of absence.

Strategic intelligence officer Steele (Elizabeth Reynolds) during the Tet Offensive.

Joe Keller (Phil Godeck) explains his authorization of a
batch of faulty cylinder heads for air force P-40s.

Ron Winter, author of *Masters of the Art: A Fighting Marine's Memoir of Vietnam*.

Officer Tepperman (Al Terry) commands prisoners
to clean the brig in a field day maneuver.

Steve Starger, playwright of *All Sunsets Look Alike*, *The Man Who Knew Trotsky*, *Slick Sleeves*, *Ned and Alyce*; musical director for *Came So Far for Beauty: The Music of Leonard Cohen*, *American Warriors*, *This is My Country*; producer of soundtrack for *Who By Fire* (2011).

2009: *This Is My Country* by Herman Shemonsky

Background

The fundraiser was a success. VMTC now had $2,000 to mount a production, a modest amount that would cover the rental of a small theater and some props and lighting instruments. The company plan had been to produce Steve Starger's *Slick Sleeves*, which had been put on hold due to inadequate theater facilities. However, now that we had funds, Herman proposed to the board that it was time for his musical, the one he had not been permitted to direct for New Britain Repertory. Steve would be the musical director, and he would be responsible for locating a theater. Steve agreed to put his show on hold for a year and to collaborate on the musical.

Herman and Clark had a decades-long history of collaboration. Clark had designed for Herman, and Herman had worked as an actor when Clark was producing. It was a natural for Herman to assume Clark would produce his show. But Clark's technical days were over. He was declining rapidly, and no longer had the stamina to participate in any activities for more than an hour or possibly two. Unfortunately, his superb technical competence could not be matched by anyone in the company.

In addition, I needed to be at home with him, and I was relieved that this was a show I would not have to manage. Herman enlisted his nephew, Barry, to produce. Although inexperienced, he worked diligently to raise money and promote the show. Herman recruited the talented Frank Veneziano to create a sound tape of audio highlights from different eras, such as original radio broadcasts, air-strike alerts, horse's hooves, etc., to enrich the narratives. However, we could not find a stage manager or costumer. As artistic director, I was obliged to step into those roles, reluctantly leaving Clark at home. No tech support was forthcoming either, and Phil took on the job of gathering, assembling, and transporting set pieces to the theater.

The company likely underestimated that Clark's loss of vitality was permanent and assumed he would provide his usual technical support. But Clark was dying and could no longer be responsible for productions.

Synopsis

This Is My Country is a full-scale musical that spans the American Revolution through Vietnam. Music from each war period was coordinated with period costuming as narrators led the audience on a historical journey. The trip began with the founding of the country and continued through early settlement, the abolition of slavery, the industrial revolution, and the information age of the twentieth century. Our opening introduced the country's struggle for independence and survival in the midst of harsh winters, famine, and infant mortality. Musical numbers included "Johnny Has Gone for a Soldier" with Bill Walach of the Morgans on mandolin, Mik Bolduc on guitar, and Steve on piano. The musical lead for the Civil War period was "The Battle Hymn of the Republic." Following this, Union and Confederate soldiers met campsite for a musical face-off. Alternately singing regional numbers such as "John Brown's Body" and "My Old Kentucky Home," they eventually collaborated on the nonpartisan number "When Johnny Comes Marching Home."

The World War I segment opened with performers joyfully dancing to "Ja-Da" until the music wound down like an old Victrola. Selections included "Keep the Home Fires Burning," "Over There," and "I'll Be Home for Christmas," in a poignant scene in which a young soldier promises his sweetheart he will be with her again. The scene ends with the delivery of a telegram of his death. The World War II lead, FDR's "Day of Infamy" speech, was mixed with sounds of sirens, bombs, artillery, calls for help, cries, aircraft engines, and machine-gun fire. Performers enter singing "Remember Pearl Harbor" and dance to "GI Jive." Narrators referenced the civil air patrol, air-raid wardens, food stamps, rations on canned goods and dairy products, war bonds, and women taking over factory jobs vacated by men who had gone to war. "In the Fuhrer's Face," sung by the company, was a song mocking Hitler.

The Korean conflict, five years after the end of World War II, was of comparatively minor significance to the American public, despite its extreme military hardship. The subzero temperatures of North Korea, foxhole warfare, and brainwashing techniques were devastating. Sometimes called the forgotten war, Korean veterans were not welcomed home as World War II warriors had been. Music from the period includes "I Believe," "Goodnight, Irene," and "Unforgettable."

Finally, the Vietnam segment opened with the track "Gimme Shelter" by the Rolling Stones. "The Ballad of the Green Berets," recorded by Staff Sergeant Barry Sadler and number one on the charts in 1966, played as solders in arms stood at attention. Additional music included "Leaving on a Jet Plane," "The Times They Are a-Changin'" and "MASH." The show finale was audience-participation number: "This Land Is Your Land."

Challenges

Barry had secured a performance space at the Mandell Jewish Community Center in West Hartford. Clark agreed to select slide projections of national flags and recognizable icons, such as the Red Cross and USO symbols, to use as a visual backdrop. He designed, with great effort, a lighting plot for the theater, although he could no longer focus the instruments or run the lighting board. Due to our anticipated need to choreograph and block timed scenes and set changes, we rented a rehearsal hall so we could seamlessly transition into the theater. Meanwhile, Phil gathered a list of props that included a wooden wagon to roll across the stage, rifles, helmets, several tree stumps, a stand-alone radio, a table with chairs, a park bench, a flip chart, a colonial flag. Publicity photos were needed, and articles to be released to the press.

Professional musicians Bill Walach on mandolin, Mick Bolduc on guitar, and Steve on piano collaborated, producing a haunting, often mournful accompaniment. Then, three weeks prior to performance, Herman lost his footing while getting out of Steve's car. He stumbled over unstable ground, landing facedown on concrete, sustaining a broken nose and leg and requiring the implant of a pacemaker. He would not return to rehearsal. Although the music and narrative portions had been rehearsed, no blocking had been established. As artistic director, I took over directing the show, while Phil relieved me by covering some rehearsal nights, organizing backstage costume changes, and assisting actors with entrance and exit cues.

Clark agreed to run the lighting board, a generous gesture but detrimental to his well being, since he could no longer concentrate or move without extraordinary fatigue.

Actors

Herman's script required a cast of twelve, performing multiple roles. Actors were required to sing, dance, and act. Elaborate costume changes delayed curtain times. Props included a life-size wagon, a tree stump, a standing radio, a large table and chairs, all to be set up and struck by the players between scenes. This could have been simplified with an adequate technical crew, which we could not provide.

For the actors, the rehearsal process was difficult. Long periods of time elapsed while cast members waited to participate. Our sudden shift in leadership undermined cast confidence that the original artistic goals would be achieved. In addition, due to the Mandell Center's availability, we had to put the show up three weeks earlier than planned. This inadvertently handicapped us with an under-rehearsed show. Considering the many shifting circumstances intrinsic to this show, the cast delivered a courageous performance.

(left to right) Gloria Gick, Sid Druckman, Heather Godeck, Elizabeth Reynolds, Emily Godeck, Shayna Gunn, Michael King, Jerilyn Rae, Wayne Riemer, Tony Enright, Jardo Opocensky Jr., and Myron Craig. Lighting and set design by Clark Bowlen.

(left to right) Elizabeth Reynolds, Jerilyn Rae, Michael King, Gloria Gick, Tony Enright, Myron Craig, Shayna Gunn, and Jardo Opocensky. Lighting and set design by Clark Bowlen.

Jerilyn Rae and Michael King sing a duet, promising one another they will be together for Christmas. Lighting and set design by Clark Bowlen.

Jardo Opocensky and Myron Craig honor the war dead as a recording of Staff Sergeant Barry Sadler's "Ballad of the Green Berets" plays. Lighting and set design by Clark Bowlen.

2010: *Slick Sleeves* by Steve Starger

Background

The VMTC board agreed that given our finite resources, our musical was an overreach. It was now clear to all that Clark was not returning. He had fallen and was in a body cast with broken ribs. Homecare services, such as nursing and physical and speech therapy, allowed Clark to remain at home. Steve had retired and relocated to Rhode Island with his wife. Herman's rehabilitation would take many months. Phil and I were committed to producing Steve's play, *Slick Sleeves*, which had been postponed for the past two years.

Phil made a presentation to the Opera House Players Board in East Windsor, which accepted our show as a guest production for the upcoming season. Clark's set and lighting design from 2008 was approved. Our rehearsal site would be Phil's large garage. Phil agreed to coach all military drills. He also acquired the numerous set pieces, including bunkers, footlockers, desks, benches and weights, weapons, and military uniforms with appropriate insignia. The Opera House allowed us to hold auditions at the theater. Our goal was to cast as many veterans as possible.

Synopsis

"Slick sleeve" is a derogatory term used to describe an inexperienced recruit. In this show, three young recruits meet in boot camp to prepare for combat service. One is a physically gifted, honorable soldier. Another is physically inept intellectual who aspires to be a field journalist. The third is an undermining bully who enjoys sabotaging his comrades. It is the duty of the drill sergeant to prepare them for combat by teaching them how to protect themselves and each other. The aspiring journalist is designated "Gomer" or scapegoat by the sergeant. The entire company is punished when he performs poorly. The lesson is that one poor performer endangers the whole. The script takes recruits through six weeks of boot camp and the ensuing emotional adaptations that transition them from civilians to soldiers. These adjustments include adhering to a strict code of conduct, self-discipline, comrade support, and high performance under pressure. These attributes are demonstrated by the sergeant in his personal encounters with the soldiers as well as the overt instruction the recruits receive.

The final post of Major Andrew Olmsted, who died in Iraq in January 2008, is included as a commentary on the action of the play. The major, played by veteran Michael Flatley, makes observations about career soldiering, the principles that inspired him, and why an army is needed. He borrows from film and other popular culture to create an eloquently argued universal soldier voice. It is an effective counterpoint to the immediacy of the script. The major exits prior to the conclusion, but remains a lingering, disembodied presence.

Challenges

The logistics of the theater move-in were difficult, especially for Phil. A heavy-duty camouflage backdrop, the full width and length of the stage, required rigging. The assembly of the bunkers and the intricate collection of military dress, properties, and equipment demanded extraordinary devotion to detail. In addition, Phil led all military drills, field exercises, and a choreographed dream sequence of military arms display I added to the show. Simulated battlefield sounds and a flashing strobe helped create D-day final boot camp requirements. Phil's wife, Danelle, took on program layout, marketing, and publicity. The production was an artistic success and the final production Clark would attend.

Actors

Veteran Al Terry played Sergeant Watkins, a tough but devoted army career man whose job it is to turn civilians into soldiers. He is relentless with his troops and torments any recruit who exhibits substandard physical aptitude. Stephen Saxton played Matt, creating a thoughtful student of war literature, bullied by his sergeant and fellow trainee. With the encouragement of his gifted comrade, Andrew, played by veteran Ben Hillard, Matt works to overcome his limitations to become a top-class graduate. The otherworldly voice of the recently deceased major provided a sobering message on the sacrifice of service. A footnote to the production is Al Terry's emotional work upon finding the poems by Siegfried Sassoon, Wilfred Owen, and Federico Garcia Lorca that Matt leaves behind in the bunkers. As Watkins begins to read, he is amazed at how much he identifies with the writing. He sits down on a bunk, absorbed in thought. He is only interrupted when he hears the sound of an incoming bus of new recruits tramping onto the base. He "straightens up and becomes a fearsome figure of a sergeant" before greeting his new trainees. This piece of silent acting was executed flawlessly.

The cast for *Slick Sleeves* could not have been better. We worked as a team and cooperatively focused on the goals at hand. I was honored to be working with such a fine group, especially as Clark, home in a hospital bed in our living room, lost more of his basic abilities to move, speak, track conversation, and perform daily life functions. Although Clark designed the set, program, poster and lighting, he only came to the theater twice—once as a lighting consultant and the second time for the performance. The Opera House Players received us quite cordially and made our work easy. Our show received television and newspaper coverage, and Phil connected with the East Windsor American Legion, which expressed interest in involving our company in educational projects.

(left to right) Lasko (Jeffrey Sirois), Andrew (Ben Hillard), Drill trainee (Myron Craig) and Matt (Stephen Saxton) stand at attention as Sergeant Watkins (Al Terry) runs drill. Major Olmsted (Michael Flatley) observes from stage left but is not seen by characters. Lighting and set design by Clark Bowlen.

Major Olmsted (Michael Flatley) speaks about the brevity of life. Lighting and set design by Clark Bowlen.

Matt (Stephen Saxton) is assisted by Sergeant Watkins (Terry) during training exercises. Lighting and set design by Clark Bowlen.

Matt (Stephen Saxton) listens as Sergeant Watkins (Terry) advises him about the rigors of military life. Lighting and set design by Clark Bowlen.

2011: *Who By Fire: Selected Scenes from Mark Baker's Nam*

Background

Our home in East Windsor was the base of VMTC's operations. When rehearsal space was unavailable, our basement served as studio. Clark, now confined to a hospital bed in our living room and requiring continuous care, could no longer be left unattended due to his paralysis. It was only serendipity that allowed us to produce our final show, *Who By Fire*, months before his death. *Slick Sleeves* had been coproduced with the Opera House Players of East Windsor.

During the run, we met with the American Legion of East Windsor, which planned to sponsor the installation of the Traveling Wall, a smaller replica of the Vietnam War Memorial, in summer 2011. The organization invited us to educate local school students about Vietnam. Most production concepts were out of the question. But a simple educational presentation, planned in our home, could work. Our 1997 veterans show, *Who By Fire*, had specifically focused on Vietnam. The memorial wall, our central image in the production, was now coming to us. Clark was once again part of our creative circle as actors read for potential roles. The company rehearsed in our basement.

Synopsis

Nam, Mark Baker's 1981 collection of interviews with Vietnam veterans, was now out of print. Our goal, this time, was to provide a range of veteran profiles and highlight the issues associated with their return. We would open a historical window. Steve Starger and I collaborated by phone to select stories about racial diversity, women, and the particular alienation that comes when entering foreign territory with an ambiguous, invisible enemy. We also addressed homeland unrest and society's distrust of returning veterans. A new recruit, played by Stephen Saxton, begins his story, progressively unfolding his combat experience in a series of monologues that are interwoven between other narratives. This device threaded disparate elements. Steve's 1960s' rock band, GC-4594, had recently released a CD featuring cuts with signature sounds of the era, which we used between sequences.

Challenges

Costumes consisted of black slacks and white shirts. A bare stage with four chairs was our performance space. The austere presentation focused on character work. Junior and senior classes met for separate performances and postperformance discussions. The students were attentive and engaged throughout performance and discussion, asking not only about VMTC, but about how veterans felt participating. Many students had active-duty or veteran family members and friends. We discussed the historic significance of the Wall and the honor the town received in displaying the installation. We encouraged students to attend the opening ceremonies, in which VMTC participated. VMTC produced the show independently at a local restaurant. Special hours were arranged for our shows and a reception followed. Clark did not attend our last production. He was, however, certainly present.

Actors

On November 2011, Clark and I assembled the company to say good-bye formally. We thanked everyone for their service and devotion to the company. Although Clark was not able to speak himself, each company member wished him farewell. Members commended Clark's continued dedication to the company despite his failing health. The gathering was a beautiful closing of our circle.

Clark died on January 8, 2012. VMTC's work was prominently displayed at his memorial—in posters, production photos, and set designs. Former students, fellow professors, community actors, veterans, producers, and directors gathered with family and friends to pay tribute to his life. People sang, recited poetry, and shared their memories of him.

Clark's courage to break from socially traditional theater was intrinsic to his personality. Always quick to shine the spotlight away from him, his humane and authentic self was his greatest asset.

Stephen Saxton describes one recruit's initiation
to warfare as Myron Craig listens.

(left to right) Kathleen Keena, Sid Druckman, and Myron Craig
take on roles as Vietnam warriors recalling their service days.

(left to right) Sid Druckman, Myron Craig, Stephen Saxton, and Kathleen Keena in an after-performance discussion of *Who By Fire* (2011).

2012: *Ned and Alyce* by Steve Starger

At Clark's memorial service, I found myself recruiting actors for VMTC's next, and possibly final, production. I wanted the material to honor Clark and also to summarize our relationship and work life. Steve had written a one act-play about two people who meet in chemotherapy treatment. They fall in love, one survives, but the other does not. Although it did not have a veterans theme, I was already thinking of making it into a movie and had requested donations in Clark's name be made to VMTC, hoping to dedicate a production in his memory. Many people loved Clark, and funds poured into the company. Although directing a video was new to me, it made sense since it would have a longer life than a stage production and could be viewed by a wider audience. Steve and I agreed that collaboration in his memory felt right since we had worked so closely as a trio over the years.

Ned and Alyce was performed by Clark's former students, Erin Fitzmaurice, Jared Ober, and Sarah Triano and completed as a labor of love. Myron Craig of VMTC became our video technician. Despite difficulties with rehearsal and shooting schedules, and within nine months of Clark's death, we finished the project. I am grateful to David Rojas, whose cinematography and screen editing was invaluable. In addition, David understood the nature of the project, offering suggestions on scene setups, lighting, and other details. The movie can be located on YouTube under *Ned and Alyce*, Kathy Keena, director.

Although VMTC continued to meet, this was our final production. The company had run its course. Clark and I had been privileged to work with many fine artists throughout the years. We were most fortunate to be life partners, professionally and personally.

Kathleen Keena, artistic director, VMTC.

Clark Bowlen, December 9, 1940 to January 8, 2012.
Manchester Community College Emeritus Professor of Communications
Award-winning Ming Cho Lee Set Designer
Shakespearian Scholar
Innovator of Social Issues and Multiracial Casting at MCC
Producer of International Premiere of a Musical Tribute to Leonard Cohen
Producer of Original Plays by Local Playwrights
Empowerment of Military Veterans via Theater
Beloved Husband

APPENDIX 1
CAME SO FAR FOR BEAUTY:
THE MUSIC OF LEONARD COHEN

Adapted by Clark Bowlen, Kathleen Keena, Deborah Simmons, and Steve Starger

Characters

Mature artist: a distinguished, reflective man in his late fifties or early sixties. He is dressed in a well-tailored suit.

Younger self: the artist twenty to thirty years ago. His dress changes as the play progresses.

Suzanne: the mature artist's muse, the perfect woman he could never find. She is dressed as described in the song "Suzanne."

Crew: three men and three women who are the mature artist's road crew. They play various parts—young man, young woman, barflies, backup singers, etc.—in scenes from his past and dress accordingly.

Original Script Development

The concept for our show began with a list of songs that Steve and I viewed as potential performance selections. Our goal was to illustrate Cohen's musical and personal evolution using my research of his writing, biographies, spiritual journey, and music.

Much like Lula and Clay in *Dutchman*, the roles in *Came So Far for Beauty* were symbols for larger concepts, represented by specific characters defining nuanced interconnections. The crew members assume multiple roles to illustrate Leonard's past experiences and interpret his lyrics and are reminiscent of a Greek chorus. When the play returns to the present, the crew members take up their original positions as backup singers on tour with Leonard Cohen. They also assist in the set strike as they pack up for their next performance.

Action Overview

The action of the play takes place on an empty stage, upon which the mature artist will give a concert later that day. Scattered about the perimeters of the stage, as if left over from previous shows, are all the props and costumes that will be used in the play. Upstage is a large mirror of the kind used by dancers, placed to reflect what happens on stage as well as the audience as they enter. It is actually a mirror scrim; when lights are turned on behind it, we see through it to the action behind as well as the reflection of what is in front of it. (Technical note: one-way, 1/8" Plexiglas works well for this effect.)

This is a memory play. Through the egis of his muse, Suzanne, who appears from behind the mirror, the mature artist remembers his career. During the action of the play, he observes and sometimes interacts with his younger self and others, played by members of the crew. Under the direction of Suzanne, who serves as stage manager of the artist's memory, the crew change properties and help actors don costumes for each scene from the past. This is done in full view of the audience and the mature artist. Once a scene from the past is over, the costumes and properties are moved backstage. In act 2, when the mature artist comes out of memory, the stage is bare.

Act 1, Scene 1 (1990s)

Mature Leonard enters the backstage dressing room to prepare for his concert tour. He is dressed in a simple tailored suit, a pared-down look. Suzanne visits him in his dressing room mirror; then he is visited by Young Leonard as he retraces his musical career. These sequences are memory/flashback/dreamlike.

During the overture, Suzanne's voice narrates, "Spring comes into Quebec." Mature Leonard sings "Came So Far for Beauty," which evokes a vision of Suzanne in the dressing-room mirror. She dances as he watches. This is the first of Leonard's memories. Suzanne evokes Young Leonard, also in the mirror, and they dance to and then sing "Suzanne," while they step from behind the mirror to center stage.

Suzanne becomes the stage manager and sings "Sisters of Mercy" as she directs the crew to set up stage for "Chelsea Hotel." Mature Leonard watches. Young Leonard enters hotel set and sings "Chelsea Hotel #2" to a crew woman who is dressed as a vaguely 1960s Janis Joplin type. Suzanne sings "Winter Lady" as the crew adjusts hotel set for "Hey, That's No Way to Say Goodbye," which Young Leonard sings with his male lover (played by a male crew member) as they part. This relationship is a deep, childhood-originated love, which devastates him and results in his shift from romanticism to cynicism and despair in the next scene. Suzanne sings "Stranger Song" as the crew resets for "Famous Blue Raincoat." During this song, Young Leonard writes to his former male lover, who has since become involved with the woman from "Chelsea Hotel." During the song, his two former lovers meet at a train station and elope as Young Leonard writes at 4:00 a.m. on a winter night.

Mature Leonard watches all of this from his dressing room.

Act 1, Scene 2

Suzanne directs the crew to set up a late 1970s country-and-western bar as she recites "It was a dance of masks." Young Leonard, very drunk, is sitting in the bar. The crew changes into barflies. Young Leonard begins "Heart With No Companion" as Mature Leonard walks in with a date. Mature Leonard listens and responds to the self-pity by advising Young

Leonard to pull himself together. Mature Leonard does this by singing "There Is a War" and challenging Young Leonard to return to it.

Young Leonard is annoyed by Mature Leonard's intervention and responds with a bawdy, obnoxious, drunk "Don't Go Home with Your Hard-On," joined by the male chorus. He sings the song to irritate and provoke Mature Leonard, directing his resentment at him. Mature Leonard responds with "Closing Time." He asks Young Leonard to remember when he is older that "it isn't worth a damn" and helps the younger man to a chair, where he collapses as the rest of the chorus join in a line dance as they sing the number. The lights go up abruptly at the end of the piece, as if the bar had just flipped on house lights.

Act 2, Scene 1

During intermission, Suzanne directs the male crew members to set up mikes and move amps, etc., in preparation for a disco concert. As disco lighting comes up from the back, Young Leonard, in a glitzy Las Vegas–style costume, enters with three disco-babe backup singers. They sing "First We Take Manhattan." His costume is overdone, a caricature. The backup singers exit, and Young Leonard sings "Leaving Green Sleeves" in a solo spot. His third number, "I'm Your Man," a solo, is unfinished as Young Leonard realizes he cannot continue to misrepresent himself. He walks off before the "I'm Your Man" refrain and meets Mature Leonard backstage. Mature Leonard helps Young Leonard take off his Las Vegas costume as the younger man collapses.

Meanwhile, Suzanne rushes to cover Young Leonard's abrupt exit by cueing the backup singers to begin the next number, "Jazz Police," without him. The performers wear black, jazzy dance costumes. The piece has been choreographed as a crisp modern dance, but the performers are thrown by the absence of Young Leonard and stumble through the lyrics, stepping on each other's lines, while trying to maintain their coolness.

Backstage, Mature Leonard sings "Everybody Knows" to Young Leonard, confirming his suspicion that people can see through him. The full road crew, now loading out the disco set, sing backup. The lights go black as a Mature Leonard recites "It Is All Around Me."

Act 2, Scene 2

Mature Leonard, center stage, sings "Waiting for the Miracle" as an explanation for having "wasted half my life away." Crew members join him in the number as they pick up their belongings—makeup kits, jackets, and bags. Suzanne watches and listens, perhaps in the mirror, but he does not see her. Young Leonard joins him to sing the "Came So Far for Beauty" reprise. Suzanne continues to watch from mirror. The two selves integrate. Young and Mature Leonard are now dressed identically. Young Leonard exits to join the chorus. Suzanne reads "Magic is Alive." Mature Leonard reenters and sings "Tower of Song," perhaps from a stage ladder, with chorus below him or at his feet.

Suzanne appears at the end of the song and invites him to dance with her in a mirror image of her opening dance with Young Leonard. They sing and dance the "Dance Me to the End of Love" reprise. The dressing room and mirror disappear. As the number ends, Mature Leonard gently directs Suzanne to a seat. He directs "Hallelujah" to her, ironically. She in turn summons the full troupe to join him in expressing that life is magnificent, though imperfect. The style is gospel, inclusive, reverent, and bittersweet. The song closes the show.

At the end of the curtain calls, the company reprises "Dance Me to the End of Love."

ACT 1, SCENE 1

> House lights to half. Overture plays. After overture, SUZANNE DL.

SUZANNE
Spring comes into Quebec from the West. It is the warm Japan current that brings the change of season to the West Coast of Canada and then the west wind picks it up. It comes across the prairies in the breath of the Chinook, waking up the grain and caves of bears. It flows over Ontario like a dream of legislation and sneaks into Quebec, into our villages, between our birch trees. In Montreal, the cafes, like a bed of tulip bulbs, sprout from their cellars in a display of awnings and chairs. In Montreal,

spring is like an autopsy. Everyone wants to see the inside of the frozen mammoth. Girls rip off their sleeves, and the flesh is sweet and white, like wood under green bark. From the streets a sexual manifesto rises like an inflating tire, "The winter has not killed us again!" Spring comes into Quebec from Japan, and like a prewar Crackerjack prize, it breaks the first day because we play with it. Spring comes to Montreal so briefly, you can name the day plan nothing for it.

Leonard Cohen, *Beautiful Losers*, 1966.

> SUZANNE disappears as MATURE ARTIST and CREW enter from back of the house. They are to prepare theater for the opening of a new concert. Ad-lib greetings, etc. As they arrive on stage, house lights dim. CREW and MATURE ARTIST inspect stage. CREW goes backstage, leaving MATURE ARTIST alone. He sings "Came So Far for Beauty." During the song, lights come up slowly to reveal SUZANNE dancing behind the mirror. He sees her. He stands DS of mirror with SUZANNE.

MATURE ARTIST sings "Came So Far for Beauty."

> Music segues into "Suzanne." SUZANNE continues to dance, summoning the Mature Artist's YOUNGER SELF. She and YOUNGER SELF dance a pas de deux behind the mirror while the pit plays one verse of "Suzanne," then comes out from behind mirror to continue the dance, and sing. MATURE ARTIST watches.

YOUNGER SELF sings "Suzanne."

SUZANNE *(begins to sing on the following lines)*
Jesus was a sailor
When he walked upon the water ...

> MATURE ARTIST mimes dancing with SUZANNE as she and YOUNGER SELF dance.

YOUNGER SELF AND SUZANNE *(continue singing)*
Now Suzanne takes your hand
And she heads you to the river ...
Leonard Cohen, Stranger Music (BMI), 1967.

> SUZANNE directs CREW to set up Chelsea Hotel set DL—a single bed, a small night table, a straight chair. It is the 1960s. It is late at night, and through a window, the light from a broken neon sign blinks on and off randomly. During the setup SUZANNE sings one or two verses of "Sisters of Mercy." MATURE ARTIST observes.

SUZANNE sings "Sisters of Mercy."
Leonard Cohen, Stranger Music (BMI), 1967.

> SUZANNE leads YOUNGER SELF and YOUNG WOMAN to their places, he on the chair, she facing away on the bed. She is in his memory. While he sings, she gets dressed, cooks heroin, shoots up, and stumbles out. SUZANNE and MATURE ARTIST watch.

> YOUNGER SELF sings "Chelsea Hotel #2."
> Leonard Cohen, Stranger Music (BMI), 1974.

> SUZANNE directs CREW to make changes to the Chelsea Hotel set. It is now early in the morning. During change, SUZANNE sings a few verses of "Winter Lady." MATURE ARTIST observes.

SUZANNE sings "Winter Lady."
Leonard Cohen, Stranger Music (BMI), 1967.

> SUZANNE leads YOUNGER SELF to the bed. YOUNG MAN enters and gets dressed. SUZANNE and MATURE ARTIST watch.

YOUNGER SELF sings "Hey That's No Way to Say Goodbye."
I'm not looking for another
As I wander in my time ...

BOTH *(sing together)*.
I loved you in the morning
our kisses deep and warm ...
Leonard Cohen, Stranger Music (BMI), 1967.

> YOUNG MAN leaves during the last verse. At end of song,
> SUZANNE directs CREW to rearrange Chelsea Hotel set.
> It is late at night again. A forlorn Christmas tree is on the
> bedside table. During change SUZANNE sings two verses of
> "Stranger Song." MATURE ARTIST observes.

SUZANNE sings "Stranger Song."
Leonard Cohen, Stranger Music (BMI), 1967.

> SUZANNE leads YOUNGER SELF to chair. He sits and
> writes a letter. SUZANNE and MATURE ARTIST watch.

> YOUNG MAN from "Hey ..." enters and sits on bench DR,
> waiting for someone.

YOUNG MAN sings "Famous Blue Raincoat."
The last time we saw you, you looked so much older.
Your famous blue raincoat was torn at the shoulder.

> YOUNG WOMAN from "Chelsea Hotel" enters and joins
> YOUNG MAN on bench.

YOUNG MAN AND YOUNG WOMAN
And when she came back she was nobody's wife.

> YOUNG MAN and YOUNG WOMAN leave together.

YOUNG MAN AND YOUNG WOMAN
I want you to know that his woman is free.
Leonard Cohen, Stranger Music (BMI), 1971.

(House to black, scene 1 out, lights up as crew clears Chelsea Hotel.)

ACT 1, SCENE 2

SUZANNE directs CREW to strike Chelsea Hotel (off-stage) and set up the bar—three round bar tables with red-and-white checked tablecloths, DL, UC, DR. Three chairs at each table. One mike, DC. It is the 1970s. When change is complete, CREW dons country-western costumes and become BARFLIES. YOUNGER SELF sits at center table, drunk and feeling sorry for himself. During the change, SUZANNE speaks to MATURE ARTIST.

SUZANNE.
I change
I am the same
I change
I am the same
I change
I am the same
I change
I am the same
I change
I am the same
I change
I am the same
He did not miss a syllable and he loved the works he sang because as he sang each sound he saw it change and every change was a return and every return was a change.
I change
I am the same

I change
I am the same
I change
I am the same
I change
I am the same
I change
I am the same
I change
I am the same
I change
I am the same.

> During the following scene, SUZANNE takes the hand of a reluctant MATURE ARTIST and leads him into the bar, seating him DR at a table next to one of the female BARFLIES.

SUZANNE
It was a dance of masks and every mask was perfect because every mask was a real face and every face was a real mask so there was no mask and there was no face for there was but one dance in which there was but one mask but one true face which was the same and which was a thing without a name which changed and changed into itself over and over. Leonard Cohen, *Beautiful Losers*, 1966.

> SUZANNE moves DL and watches action throughout the balance of the act.

> YOUNGER SELF (with great self pity) sings "Heart with No Companion." MATURE ARTIST sets YOUNGER SELF straight.

YOUNGER SELF *(spoken to MATURE ARTIST)*
To the days of shame that are coming
To the nights of wild distress.
Though your promise counts for nothing,
You must keep it nonetheless.

MATURE ARTIST *(facing down YOUNGER SELF)*.
Why don't you come back to the war—
Pick up your tiny burden?
Leonard Cohen, *1074*, Stranger Music (BMI), 1988.

> YOUNGER SELF sings "Don't Go Home with Your Hard-On."
> Very drunk, he rounds up the male BARFLIES, and they
> stumble to the mike.
> Leonard Cohen, Stranger Music (BMI), 1977.

YOUNGER SELF *(defiant, for MATURE ARTIST'S benefit)*.
I was born in a beauty salon

YOUNGER SELF, MALE BARFLIES.
But don't go home with your hard-on

YOUNGER SELF
I've looked behind all these faces

> Chorus is repeated several times, wildly, with group.

MATURE ARTIST sings "Closing Time" *(having the final word)*.
Leonard Cohen, Stranger Music (BMI), 1992.

> The BARFLIES begin a line dance. All except YOUNGER
> SELF sing.

ALL
All the women tear their blouses off ...

BARFLIES
We're lonely, we're romantic …

> Male and female BARFLY do a solo dance for one instrumental verse.

MATURE ARTIST
We're drinking and we're dancing …

ALL
And the whole damn place goes crazy twice …

> On the final note, lighting abruptly shifts to full brightness. Barflies freeze. Suzanne comes DS, takes MATURE ARTIST's hand and leads him silently through the bar, past BARFLIES and YOUNGER SELF, and off-stage behind the mirror. Stage fades to black.

ACT 2, SCENE 1

> During the intermission the CREW clears (off-stage) the tables and chairs from the bar scene and the MALE CREW set three mikes DS, do mike checks, etc. At the end of intermission, SUZANNE comes from behind the mirror and does one last mike check; then, as she disappears behind the mirror, the house and stage lights go to black.

> During the blackout, the FEMALE BACKUP SINGERS take their places, one behind each mike, with YOUNGER SELF, DC. MATURE ARTIST and SUZANNE are US in front of the mirror.

> It is the early 1980s. It is the opening of YOUNGER SELF's concert. He is dressed like Tom Jones, the FEMALE BACKUP SINGERS are sexy and glitzy. There is a mirror ball, and

lights pulse to the beat of the music. YOUNGER SELF is trying too hard to project power and sexuality.

The pit plays an introduction in the black, and lights pop up to reveal YOUNGER SELF and the FEMALE BACKUP SINGERS facing upstage, moving to the beat.

YOUNGER SELF *(turns to face the audience)* sings "First We Take Manhattan."

ALL *(Backup singers, who have been facing upstage, turn to face audience)*.
First we take Manhattan, then we take Berlin.

YOUNGER SELF
I'm guided by a signal in the heavens.
Leonard Cohen, Stranger Music (BMI), 1988.

They spin, face upstage, and freeze. Blackout.

During the blackout, SUZANNE strikes the left and right mikes; the performers group themselves around one mike with YOUNGER SELF in the middle. The concert continues. YOUNGER SELF sings seductively, directing one stanza to each of the three FEMALE BACKUP SINGERS. MATURE ARTIST and SUZANNE are US in the front of the mirror.

YOUNGER SELF sings "Leaving Green Sleeves."

ALL
Green sleeves, you're all alone.

YOUNGER SELF
I sang my songs. I told my lies.
Leonard Cohen, Stranger Music (BMI), 1974.

Lights fade to black, FEMALE BACKUP SINGERS exit. SUZANNE places small bench DLC, on which YOUNGER SELF suggestively drapes himself. Lights come up. MATURE ARTIST and SUZANNE are US in front of the mirror.

YOUNGER SELF sings "I'm Your Man." *(Overtly sexy, perhaps painfully so. During the song he becomes increasingly self-conscious.)*
… Or if you want to take me
For a ride
You know you … *(Drops mike, angrily walks off stage.)*
Leonard Cohen, Stranger Music (BMI), 1988.

YOUNGER SELF, who has been struggling throughout the concert to maintain his "Tom Jones" posture, stops midsong, looks at audience and at himself, and storms offstage, discarding his costume as he goes.

The pit continues to play. He "enters" the backstage area, glares at MATURE ARTIST, sits at the makeup table, and angrily stares at himself in the mirror. Throughout, the pit vamps in confusion.

SUZANNE runs on in a panic, looks at audience, and then strikes the bench for lack of anything to do. She then signals the pit to go on to next number and rushes off-stage to drag the MALE AND FEMALE BACKUP SINGERS on stage to begin the next number. They are in disarray, still putting on costumes (modern-dance, sexy tights and accessories). They struggle to begin this dance number without the YOUNGER SELF, adlibbing whispers, looks, etc. There are several false starts. They get tangled in the costumes they are still putting on and begin to dance out of sync. MATURE ARTIST and SUZANNE watch from US in front of the mirror.

ALL sing "Jazz Police."

FEMALE BACKUP SINGERS
Jazz police, I hear you calling.

ALL
Wild as any freedom-loving racist,
I applaud the actions of the Chief.
Leonard Cohen, Stranger Music (BMI), 1988.

> Blackout

> The concert is over. The lights come up and the CREW,
> during the musical introduction, comes on to begin the strike
> under Suzanne's direction. US, MATURE ARTIST helps
> YOUNGER SELF remove the last of the Tom Jones outfit and
> don his street clothes, which match those of the MATURE
> ARTIST.

MATURE ARTIST sings "Everybody Knows" *(to YOUNGER SELF, setting
him straight, as they both move DS).*
Everybody knows that the dice are loaded ...
Everybody wants a box of chocolates
And a long-stemmed rose.

CREW *(joins in, also singing to YOUNGER SELF).*
Everybody knows. Everybody knows.

CREW *(still singing to YOUNGER SELF as SUZANNE leads him off stage).*
He joins in singing the last couple of bars.
Leonard Cohen and Sharon Robinson, Stranger Music (BMI) and Robinhill
Music (ASCAP), 1988.

CREW and MATURE ARTIST *(CREW leaves stage as song fades out).*

> Fade out.

The stage is now bare. Alone, the MATURE ARTIST, barely seen, prays. Introduction to "Waiting for the Miracle" vamps underneath.

MATURE ARTIST
It is all around me, the darkness. You are my only shield. Your name is my only light. What I love I have, your law is the source, this dead love that remembers only its name, yet the name is enough to open itself like a mouth, to call the dew, and drink. O dead name that through your mercy speaks to the living name, mercy harkening to the will that is bent toward it, the will whose strength is its pledge to you. O name of love, draw down the blessings of completion on the man you have cut in half to know you. Leonard Cohen, *The Book of Mercy*, 1984.

Light to black. Scene out.

ACT 2, SCENE 2

MATURE ARTIST is on stage alone as the lights come up. CREW appears dimly lit behind the mirror. They sing backup while doing a slow-motion fantasy dance/movement.

MATURE ARTIST sings "Waiting for the Miracle."
Leonard Cohen, Stranger Music (BMI), 1992.

Lights fade behind mirror, and then come up again, revealing YOUNGER SELF behind mirror. He sings with MATURE ARTIST, who stands in front of the mirror in such a way that his reflection seems to be opposite the YOUNGER SELF behind the mirror. They sing back and forth, and finally as a duet, as if integrating the aspects of each other.

YOUNGER SELF sings "Came So Far for Beauty" (reprise).
I came so far for beauty
I left so much behind

MATURE ARTIST
I thought I'd be rewarded
For such a lonely choice …
Leonard Cohen, Stranger Music (BMI), 1979.

> SUZANNE appears behind the mirror and ushers YOUNGER
> SELF off, then recites the following as the introduction to
> "Dance Me … " vamps underneath.

SUZANNE sings "Magic Is Alive."
G-D is alive. Magic is afoot. G-D is alive. Magic is a foot. G-D is a foot.
Magic is alive. Alive is a foot. Magic never died. G-d never sickened.
Many poor men lied. Many sick men lied. Magic never weakened. Magic
never hid. Magic always ruled. G-d is a foot. G-d never died. G-d was ruler
though his funeral lengthened. Though his mourners thickened. Magic
never fled. Though his shrouds were hoisted the naked G-d did live.
Leonard Cohen, *Beautiful Losers*, 1966.

> SUZANNE sings from behind mirror the MATURE ARTIST
> from in front of it.

MATURE ARTIST sings "Dance Me to the End of Love."

SUZANNE
Let me see your beauty
When the witnesses are gone

> MATURE ARTIST beckons to her, and SUZANNE comes
> out from behind the mirror and joins him C.

BOTH
Show me slowly what I only
Know the limits of

MATURE ARTIST and SUZANNE dance silently to a Klezmer violin solo for two verses, then sing the last line of the second verse.
Leonard Cohen, Stranger Music (BMI), 1984.

SUZANNE disappears behind the mirror. MATURE ARTIST is left alone on stage.

During the song, CREW comes on stage and begins cleaning up, removing the last of the props and masking the mirror. They are loading out at the end of the MATURE ARTIST's concert. They wear the costumes they wore at the beginning of the play. (Note: Black "Came So Far for Beauty" tour Crew T-shirts, work pants.)

MATURE ARTIST is left alone on a bare stage. He sings directly to the audience. The CREW, backstage, hears him start the song, and they come back in to join him. This is his and their signature tune.

MATURE ARTIST sings "Tower of Song" (*alone*).

CREW begins filtering in, one by one.

MATURE ARTIST sings to them.
I was born like this, I had no choice.

Some CREW begin to exit. Others mask mirror in preparation for packing.

MATURE ARTIST
I see standing on the other side …
Leonard Cohen, Stranger Music (BMI), 1988.

MATURE ARTIST sings "Hallelujah."

ALL
Hallelujah! Hallelujah! Hallelujah! Hallelujah!

MATURE ARTIST
Your faith was strong but you needed proof.

ALL
Hallelujah! Hallelujah! Hallelujah! Hallelujah!
Leonard Cohen, Stranger Music (BMI), 1988.

Blackout.

Finale.

In the black, the pit begins the "Dance Me to the End of Love"
reprise. Lights up, and as cast takes curtain calls, the music
gradually builds.

The cast sings "La la, la la, la, la la."

When the calls are finished, the cast erupts into a hora, which
builds energy until it spills off the stage, and the cast exits up
the aisles.

APPENDIX 2

JACQUES BREL IS ALIVE AND WELL

Narrative by Kathleen Keena
Narrated by Herman Shemonsky

4 men
2 women
Narrator (who also sings) male
Pianist (who also sings and acts) female

ACT 1

Dark stage. Brel sings "If We Only Have Love" in French. As lights come up, a screen projection of Brel can be seen center stage overhead.
Note: The screen projections will show Brel in various attitudes and stages of his life, which parallel the music.

Six bar stools are arranged in a horseshoe half-circle center stage. Downstage is performance space. Stage left is grand piano and narrator podium. Pianist enters house right in dark. Narrator, on stage at podium, begins.

NARRATOR *(unseen, voice heard in darkness)*
You are listening to Jacques Brel singing "If We only Have Love." Good evening. Brel inspired a generation including Leonard Cohen, Judy Collins, and Ray Charles. His music appealed to a broad range of international singers and audiences. Brel died at 49.

> Lights come up; narrator is now visible.

NARRATOR
Brel was a cabaret singer. His songs were translated into English by American producers Shuman and Blau, who opened the musical "Jacques Brel is Alive and Well and Living in Paris" in 1968 in Greenwich Village as a tribute to his work. Much of his music is fifty or so years old. We are performing the songs in an "emotionally" chronological order, which will tell the story of Brel's journey through life. Brel was born in Belgium and lived under Nazi occupation. His songs tell us he was acutely aware of human shortcomings. We believe Jacques Brel music is relevant, more than ever, today, as we struggle with contemporary unrest in the Middle East and society's missing essential human connections.

> The company hums "If We Only Have Love" as the narrator speaks. They enter stage right and take their places on the six barstools.

INTRODUCTION

BRUSSELS

> An energetic piece by the entire assembled company, now center stage, who sing the song to tell the story to the audience. Company members interact with each other; the dramatic goal is to convey to the audience a sense of the vitality of place. Actors may break conventional performance with direct eye contact to specific audience members to allow a more intimate cabaret experience. The number will be choreographed.

CHILDHOOD AND INNOCENCE

NARRATOR
It was a time of acceleration and change. The twentieth century endured two world wars. Rapid industrialization, nationalistic zeal ravaged the world. Let's let Brel take us back to a time when we all began in innocence.

SONS OF

> "Sons of" is sung by a mature female vocalist, backed up by three men, mix of young and mature. She comes forward after the "Brussels" number, as if wanting to explain more fully.

> Piano accompanies narrator as he introduces the next number.

NARRATOR
Children grow to become young adults and enter an unforgettable time of romantic love. But even in the bliss of waiting for Madeleine, Brel foreshadows disappointment, because "Madeleine, she never came."

MADELEINE

> The four men line up in ensemble, barbershop-quartet style, enthusiastic, wearing straw hats. Can be poorly acted; should look exaggerated.

> They sing "Madeleine," with harmonies, for comic affect.

YOUNG ADULTHOOD

NARRATOR
So, what does a young person look for in a partner? The bachelor we are about to hear from has some pretty unrealistic expectations!

THE BACHELOR'S DANCE

> Male solo dance and song number. The female dancers will "woo" him with feather fans, recalling 1930s musical films, as he sings "No, it isn't you" to both women in different stanzas of the song. On the third verse, he dances over to the pianist, kneels on one knee, and delivers flowers to her as he says "the girl who'll marry me."

> Blackout. Beat. Lights up.

NARRATOR
Inevitably, each of us must come to terms with loneliness. "Alone" and "You're Not Alone" express our universal need for connection with one another.

ALONE/YOU'RE NOT ALONE

> "Alone/You're Not Alone" duet, sung by male and female pair, back to back or on opposite corners of the stage. The tension of an argument should be sustained. A gradual move toward each other must be organic, not forced, and motivated by the sensibility of the singers hearing each other.

SINGERS
We'll do it if we can, love,
We'll do it if we can.

> Lights to half. Couple returns to their seats as female soloist takes barstool to front center stage. Single spot, tighten to cabaret tragedy level.

NARRATOR
Our next number, "I Loved," tells about first love from a woman's perspective.

I LOVED

Female soloist on barstool with single spot sings "I Loved."

NARRATOR

Oh, yes, men feel it too.

FANETTE

Male soloist with coat over one shoulder, walking on imaginary beach, sings "Fanette." Behind him, in tableau, a man and woman are posed to waltz. As music begins, they waltz elegantly CS, SR to SL, using maximum floor space as soloist stands DR and glances at them as he sings, sharing the story, which is his.

Lights to half.

NARRATOR

Our next number, originally called "Mathilde" and sung by a man, is sung by a woman in our version. Nicolas becomes her beloved's name. As the scene opens, her mother waits for her to come home; the young woman rushes in with a letter nearly knocking her mother off her feet. Her friends gather around her and try to advise restraint. She is joyful, bossy, anxious, and contradictory. Sound familiar?

MATHILDE (NICHOLAS)

Female soloist enters CS with letter, rushes toward older female cast member (her mother) addressing her. Her crowd of friends stand in the background, listening, and she eventually addresses them, explaining why she must return to the relationship that almost destroyed her earlier. She sings "Mathilde" ("Nicholas").

Blackout.

NARRATOR

And now, the exquisitely written "If You Go Away," for which Brel is best known in America.

IF YOU GO AWAY

> Narrator steps out from behind podium and sings "If You Go Away" with infinite longing. Then he walks thoughtfully back to his podium and pauses, resuming his role.

NARRATOR

Our next two numbers take us into Brel's view of a constantly changing, frenzied world. There is a chaotic tone to both numbers, reflecting the political uncertainty of the times and the personal powerlessness he felt.

MARATHON

> Entire company sings "Marathon." Should have a frantic, compulsive quality. Morally ambiguous. "Hitler" is sung as cheerfully as "Siegfried Follies." Couples dance, starting with the Charleston and updating with appropriate era dancing, but find they can't keep up with lyrics. Cast is out of breath, tempo becomes frenzied, words jumble together, until company collapses together on stage from dizziness and confusion.

> Lights to half; actors form circle for "Carousel."

NARRATOR

Brel had a way of infusing emotion into a song so that its core feeling could be understood, not just from the words, but also with the rhythm, melody, pace, and passion of delivery. "Carousel" is like "Marathon" in the relentlessness of its push, providing a feeling of people as statues stationed in space. This image is one that is apt during the Nazi occupation, and Brel's metaphors for chaos are thinly veiled.

CAROUSEL

> Entire company forms a circle on stage and sings "Carousel." Each person is carousel horse, going up and down as the group rotates in a circle. When actors are close to downstage center, their voices are loud. As they move upstage center, their voices fade to suggest distance. Thus, loudest singing is always heard downstage from various actors as they pass in front of audience.

> Blackout. Actors clear stage. End of Act 1. House lights up.

ACT 2

SOCIETY'S OUTCASTS

NARRATOR
Welcome back. Brel had an affinity for the alienated of society. His songs reflect this in many ways. He saw and felt the anguish of those who didn't fit in neatly with others. In this first number, you are about to meet Jacques Brel, "cosmic clown." Brel used exaggeration to describe some of our less than honorable impulses. Let's listen to his comic side.

JACKIE

> Solo male explains his revenge plan after being betrayed by the world in the song "Jackie." He is embittered but also playfully self-mocking and aware of his own hypocrisy.

NARRATOR
Although "Jackie" is farce, Brel's tone shifts to pathos in our next piece about a homeless wanderer.

TIMID FRIEDA

A solo woman, wanders onstage with pieces of luggage, sings "Timid Frieda." Ensemble members are grouped in couples or busy on their way to appointments, etc., as she delivers song to different townspeople, who ignore her.

NARRATOR

And now, possibly Brel's darkest song. In "Amsterdam," we are in the company of drinking sailors, women being exploited by men, gluttons eating fish heads and belching. The "rancid sound of the accordion" evokes a particularly cruel and alien atmosphere. Can you see a veil of dirty water, fog, and night? Try.

AMSTERDAM

Lights remain low, almost in blackout for "Amsterdam." Male soloist is heard offstage for two verses until pace grows more frenzied and animalistic. Singer enters from audience aisle, finds his way onto front of house from audience. Lights stay at half, so audience is surprised a live singer is near the stage; the impression is that they are listening to a recording. Soloist is dressed in sailor cap and scarf, poses on stage steps for end of song.

DISPLACED VIOLENCE

NARRATOR

Our next two numbers deal with violence. The first is about the violence that the army imposes on its warriors in preparation for the brutality and anonymity of combat. Soldiers, stripped and identities lost, stand in lines in which they are interchangeable. Brel's anger stands out against it all as defiant outrage.

NEXT

>All males in company sing "Next." One male soloist sings; the others, dressed in identical army shirts or caps, sing backup. They arrange themselves at attention, in drill formation, at ease, etc., as the singer tells his story.

NARRATOR

Jacques Brel was outraged at the slaughter of war. He used the metaphor of bullfighting to describe warfare. At bullfights, the bulls are summoned. They bleed, and the crowd goes wild. Brel compares this public display of gratuitous violence to Carthage, Waterloo, Verdun, Stalingrad, Iwo Jima, Hiroshima, Saigon, and to these we have added Baghdad.

THE BULLS

>Same male cast as "Next," but a different soloist. "The Bulls" is sung by a captain, who explains the basic training of soldiers. Upstage, cadets go through drill training, including marching, moving supplies, and rifle drills in formation.

GRIEF

NARRATOR

Although Brel did not live a long life; he was an astute observer of different life stages and mortality. Perhaps living in a time of great human suffering, terror and man's savageness to fellow man gave him this awareness.

OLD FOLKS

>Female soloist in single spot sings "Old Folks."

NARRATOR

Brel also felt the grief of others as their loved ones die.

MARIEKE

> Female soloist with guitar accompaniment and two female backup singers. They sing "Marieke." Soloist enters with box of mementos from her beloved in the service. The final one is an official death notice from the government.

DEATH

NARRATOR
Even facing his own death, Brel finds something ironic, ridiculous, and profoundly defiant to say.

FUNERAL TANGO

> Entire company sings "Funeral Tango." Soloist. Casket is placed downstage. Center stage a reception line forms of all company members. Table with food and drink is upstage right and mourners help themselves to refreshments as soloist watches. A floral arrangement is downstage right until soloist picks up flowers, closes casket, handing floral arrangement to a mourner to place on top of his casket when it closes.

NARRATOR
And now, we hear Brel's own conversation with death.

MY DEATH

> Possibly before a mirror, or a portrait of a loved one. "My Death" is the biggest solo of the evening, and company backs up soloist with harmony from their seated positions on stage as a single spot shines on him.

LOVE

NARRATOR

We wish to thank you for your kind attention. It has been an honor to be with you tonight. We leave you with Brel's belief in the power of love to transcend human imperfection. The company invites you to sing the final reprise of "If We Only Have Love" with us. Lyrics are found in your program.

IF WE ONLY HAVE LOVE

> Entire company sings "If We Only Have Love." Number begins down stage center; then company comes down stage left and stage right into audience aisles to form a circle around audience members. (Three company members on left, three on right.) Audience is invited to sing with the company.

AUDIENCE

If we only have love, then we'll only be men;
… Then with nothing at all, but the little we are,
We'll have conquered all time, all space,
The sun and the stars.

> Company joins audience, repeating last verse as they continue to sing.

> For the curtain call, company returns to stage, signaling "thank you" as if blowing a kiss to audience.

> Blackout. Lights up. Curtain call. Individual performers.

> Finale. House lights up.

BIBLIOGRAPHY

Adler, Stella. *The Technique of Acting.* New York: Bantam Books, 1988.

Ball, David. *Backwards and Forwards.* Carbondale: Southern Illinois University Press, 1983.

Baker, Mark, Ed. *Nam.* New York: William Morrow and Company, Inc., 1981.

Brook, Peter. *The Empty Space.* New York: Atheneum Publishers, 1968.

Carroll, Andrew, Ed. *Behind The Lines.* New York: Scribner, 2005.

_____. *War Letters.* New York: Scribner, 2001.

Cohen, Leonard. *Beautiful Losers.* New York and Toronto: Viking Press, Inc., and McClelland and Stewart Limited, 1966.

_____. *Book of Mercy.* Toronto: McClelland and Stewart, Inc., 1984.

_____. *Selected Poems, 1956--1968.* New York: Viking Press, Inc., 1968.

_____. *Stranger Music.* Toronto: McClelland and Stewart, Inc., 1993.

_____. *The Favourite Game.* Toronto: McClelland and Stewart, Inc. 1963.

Cushman, Robert. *Fifty Seasons at Stratford.* Toronto: Madison Press Books, 2002.

Donle, Harold. "Ambush" (unpublished narrative, 1997).

_____. "The Barber" (unpublished narrative, 1997).

Edelstein, T. J., ed. *The Stage Is All the World: The Theatrical Designs of Tanya Moiseiwitsch.* Chicago and Seattle: University of Chicago in association with the University of Washington Press, 1994.

Epstein, Helen. *Joe Papp: An American Life.* Boston and Toronto: Little Brown and Company, 1994.

Gelb, Arthur, and Barbara Gelb. *O'Neill.* New York and Toronto: Harper and Row and Fitzhenry and Whiteside, 1962.

Goldsmith, Oliver. *She Stoops to Conquer.* Garden City, NY: Fireside Theatre Library, 1976. Originally produced 1773, Covent Garden.

Guthrie, Tyrone. *A Life in the Theatre.* New York: McGraw-Hill, 1959.

Hayman, Ronald. *How to Read a Play.* London: Methuen Paperback, 1984.

Henley, Beth. *Crimes of the Heart.* New York: Dramatists Play Service, 1981.

Jones, LeRoi. *Dutchman.* New York: Apollo Editions and William Morrow, 1964.

Karnow, Stanley. *Vietnam: A History.* New York: Viking Books, 1983.

Keena, Kathleen. "Jacquel Brel narrative text for 2005 MCC production" (unpublished, 2005).

Knight, G. Wilson. *The Wheel of Fire.* New York: Methuen and Company, 1986. First published 1930 by Oxford University Press.

Laura, Shirley. *A Piece of My Heart.* New York: Samuel French, 1988.

McLure, James. *Laundry and Bourbon.* New York: Dramatists Play Service, 1981.

_____. *Lone Star.* New York: Dramatists Play Service, 1980.

_____. *Pvt. Wars.* New York: Dramatists Play Service, 1990.

Miller, Arthur. All My Sons. In *Three Plays About Business in America.* Edited by Joseph Mersand. New York: Washington Square Press, 1964.

Nadel, Ira B. *Leonard Cohen: A Life in Art.* Toronto: ECW Press, 1994.

_____. *Various Positions: A Life of Leonard Cohen.* Toronto: Random House of Canada Ltd., 1996.

Nash, N. Richard. *The Rainmaker.* New York: Samuel French, 1954.

O'Brian, Tim. *The Things They Carried.* New York: Penguin Books, 1990.

O'Neill, Eugene. *Desire Under the Elms.* In *Three Plays of Eugene O'Neill.* New York: Vintage Books and Random House, 1959.

Prochnau, William. *Once Upon a Distant War.* New York: Random House, 1995.

Scobie, Stephen, ed. *Intricate Preparations: Writing Leonard Cohen.* Toronto: ECW Press, 2000.

Shakespeare, William. *A Midsummer Night's Dream.* Edited by David Bevington. New York: Bantam Doubleday Dell, 1988.

_____. *The Taming of the Shrew.* Edited by Robert B. Heilman. New York: Signet Classic Shakespeare and New American Library, 1966.

Shanley, John Patrick. *Italian American Reconciliation*. New York: Dramatists Play Service, 1989.

Shemonsky, Herman. "This Is My Country" (unpublished, 2009).

Shepard, Sam. *Buried Child*. New York: Dramatists Play Service, 1977.

Sherriff, R.C. *Journey's End*. London: Samuel French, 1929.

Stanislavski, Constantin. *An Actor Prepares*. New York: Theatre Arts, 1936.

Spolin, Viola. *Improvisation for the Theater*. Evanston, IL: Northwestern University Press, 1963.

Starger, Stephen. "All Sunsets Look Alike" (unpublished, 1994).

_____. "ESL Class for Vietnam Combat Prep" (unpublished, 1977).

_____. "Ned and Alyce" (unpublished, 2012).

_____. "Slick Sleeves" (unpublished, 2010).

_____. "The Man Who Knew Trotsky" (unpublished, 1996).

Trudeau, G. B. *Doonesbury: The War Years*. New York: Gramercy Books and Random House, 2006.

Vineberg, Steve. *Method Actors*. New York: Schirmer Books, 1991.

Wilde, Oscar. *The Importance of Being Earnest*. New York: Samuel French, 2011.

Williams, Tennessee. *The Glass Menagerie*. New York: Dramatists Play Service, 1945.

Winter, Ronald E. *Masters of the Art*. New York: Presidio Press and Random House, 2005.

KATHLEEN KEENA

Directing

Truth in Fiction. Staged reading, Suffield Players, Suffield, CT, 2014

Ned and Alyce. Film, Veterans Memorial Theatre Company, 2012

Who By Fire. Play, Veterans Memorial Theatre Company, At the Dam Restaurant, Broad Brook, CT, 2011

Slick Sleeves. Play, Veterans Memorial Theatre Company, Opera House Players, Broad Brook, CT, 2010

This is My Country. Play, Veterans Memorial Theatre Company, Mandell Jewish Center, West Hartford, CT, 2009; alternate

American Warriors. Play, Veterans Memorial Theatre Company, Adath Israel Synagogue, Middletown, CT, 2009

Pvt. Wars. Play, Veterans Memorial Theatre Company and Connecticut Heritage Productions, Middletown, CT, 2008

Italian American Reconciliation. Play, New Britain Repertory Company, CT, 2006

Pvt. Wars. Play, Manchester Community College, Manchester, CT, 2006

The Rainmaker. Play, New Britain Repertory Company, CT, 2005

Jacques Brel Is Alive and Well. Musical, Manchester Community College, CT, 2005. Codirector with Herman Shemonsky

The Importance of Being Earnest. Play, Suffield Players, Suffield, CT, 2003

Crimes of the Heart. Play, Mark Twain Masquers, Hartford, CT, 2001

She Stoops to Conquer. Play, Manchester Community College, CT, 2001

Lone Star/Laundry and Bourbon. Play, Manchester Community College, CT, 2001

Came So Far for Beauty: The Music of Leonard Cohen. Musical, Manchester Community College, CT, 1998

Who By Fire. Play, Manchester Community College, CT, 1997

Who By Fire touring company. Play, West Haven Veterans Administration, Rocky Hill Veterans Administration, Loomis Chaffee Private School, Windsor, CT, 1997

The Man Who Knew Trotsky. Play, Manchester Community College, CT, 1994

Dutchman. Play, Naugatuck Valley Community College and Manchester Community College, CT, 1994

All Sunsets Look Alike. Play, Manchester Community College, CT, 1994

Hurston on Hurston. Play, Naugatuck Valley Community College, CT, 1994

Observing Race. Play, Manchester Community College, CT, 1993

Aids and Us. Film, Charter Oak Health Center, Hartford, CT, 1993

Romeo and Juliet. Play, Shakespeare Hartford, Hartford, CT, 1993; consultant to director Lucy Hurston

A Midsummer Night's Dream. Play, Shakespeare Hartford and Manchester Community College, CT, 1992

The Taming of the Shrew. Play, Shakespeare Hartford, Hartford, CT, 1991

Buried Child. Play, Manchester Community College, CT, 1990

Duck Variations. Play, Manchester Community College, CT, 1990

The Glass Menagerie. Play, Manchester Community College, CT, 1989

Board Memberships

Artistic director, Veterans Memorial Theatre Company, 2009–12

Newsletter editor and secretary, New Britain Repertory Company, 2006–7

Artistic director, Veterans Theater for Healing, 1997–98

Artistic director, Shakespeare Hartford, 1991–94

Artistic director, Calliope Feminist Theater Collective, 1980–82

Teaching

Manchester Community College, 1987–94.
> Advanced Acting: social issues, course development
> Minority Drama: course development
> American Drama: course development
> Introduction to Acting
> Advanced Acting

Training

Psychodrama Institute of New Haven, 1994–96

Master of arts, counseling, Saint Joseph University, summa cum laude, 1994

Master of arts, English literature, Distinguished Scholar, Central Connecticut State University, 1988

Bachelor of general studies, writing and social issues, University of Connecticut, 1986

Lee Strasberg Theater Institute, Los Angeles, 1975–76

Hartford Stage with Henry Thomas, 1974

Performances

"Toaster", *Who By Fire,* monologue, VMTC, 2012

"Miss America", *Who By Fire,* monologue, VMTC, 2012

Lula, *Dutchman,* Naugatuck Valley Community College and Manchester Community College, 1995

April Havens, *Tropical Blues,* Wesleyan University, 1993

Abbie in *Desire Under the Elms,* Manchester Community College, 1987

Selected roles, *Spoon River Anthology,* Manchester Community College, 1987

Ismene, *An Evening of Classical Women,* Connecticut Public Theater Corporation, 1980

Various improvisation roles, Calliope Feminist Collective, 1980–82

Various roles, *A Lesson in Dead Language,* Los Angeles, 1975

Various roles, *Calm Down, Mother,* Wooden Ships, 1974

Printed in the United States
By Bookmasters